INTRODUCTION TO
ITALIAN POETRY

INTRODUCTION TO ITALIAN POETRY
A Dual-Language Book

EDITED BY
Luciano Rebay

DOVER PUBLICATIONS, INC.
New York

Published in Canada by General Publishing Company, Ltd., 30 Lesmill Road, Don Mills, Toronto, Ontario.
Published in the United Kingdom by Constable and Company, Ltd., 3 The Lanchesters, 162–164 Fulham Palace Road, London W6 9ER.

This Dover edition, first published in 1991, is an unabridged and updated republication of the work originally published under the title *Invitation to Italian Poetry* by Dover Publications, Inc., New York, 1969.
This edition is also published together with a cassette entitled *Listen & Enjoy Italian Poetry* (ISBN: 0-486-99930-0).

The following poems in this collection are reprinted by special permission: "Veglia," "Senza più peso" and "Tu ti spezzasti" by Giuseppe Ungaretti; "Antico inverno" and "Uomo del mio tempo" by Salvatore Quasimodo: all by permission of Arnoldo Mondadori, Editore, Milan.
The Italian text of "Meriggiare pallido e assorto," "La casa dei doganieri" and "L'anguilla" by Eugenio Montale, by permission of Arnoldo Mondadori, Editore. The English translations, prepared specially for Dover, are used by permission of New Directions Publishing Corporation, publishers of Eugenio Montale's *Selected Poems*.

Manufactured in the United States of America
Dover Publications, Inc., 31 East 2nd Street, Mineola, N.Y. 11501

Library of Congress Cataloging-in-Publication Data

Invitation to Italian poetry.
    Introduction to Italian poetry / edited by Luciano Rebay. — Dover ed.
        p.   cm. — (A Dual-language book)
    Previously published as: Invitation to Italian poetry.
    ISBN 0-486-26715-6
    1. Italian poetry—Translations into English. 2. English poetry—Translations from Italian. 3. Italian poetry—History and criticism. 4. Poets, Italian—Biography. 5. Italian poetry. I. Rebay, Luciano. II. Title. III. Series.
PQ4208.I68   1991
851.008—dc20   90-23243
                                                                              CIP

CONTENTS

INTRODUCTION

THIS selective anthology is an introduction to some of the highlights of more than seven centuries of Italian poetry. It is intended for those who would like to acquire a degree of familiarity with the whole range of this rich literary tradition, especially students of Italian language and literature; yet many features of the anthology make it useful to lovers of poetry who know little or no Italian.

Appearing in chronological order, there are thirty-four examples of Italian verse in the original text with English translation on the opposite page. Twenty-one poets are represented, from Saint Francis of Assisi, author of the first memorable Italian lyric, "Cantico delle creature," probably composed in 1224, to Salvatore Quasimodo, winner of the 1959 Nobel Prize for Literature. A glance at the table of contents will reveal that along with the names one expects to find in any such collection—masters like Dante, Petrarch, Ariosto, Tasso, Leopardi, Foscolo, D'Annunzio, Ungaretti, Montale—are those of poets with whom the non-specialist or beginning student may not be acquainted, yet whose distinctive lyric qualities deserve to be better known: the enigmatic Compiuta Donzella, the delicate Cavalcanti, the fiery Angiolieri, the gregarious Sacchetti, the refined Poliziano, the witty Berni. Also included are figures whose outstanding achievements are not primarily associated with the art of poetry, such as Boccaccio, Lorenzo de' Medici, and Michelangelo. They have a place in this volume not only for the intrinsic value of their contributions but also because they bear evidence to the fact that Italians with artistic inclinations have always sought to master lyric poetry and that this medium of expression is a vital part of Italy's legacy to the civilization of the Western world.

A brief note introduces each poet in this collection, providing essential biographical and bibliographical data and attempting to place him in critical perspective. Thus it is hoped the reader will have a general view of the development of Italian poetry from its origins to our day. This development, it should be noted, was markedly affected by "schools" and trends such as the *dolce stil nuovo*, Petrarchism, Marinism, and hermeticism, but to only a small degree by changes in the Italian language itself. Indeed, one of the characteristics of Italian literature is the remarkable uniformity of a language which from the thirteenth century to the present time has undergone relatively minor changes. The Italian of today's poetry is still basically the same as that used by Dante in the *Divine Comedy*.

With the exceptions of the episodes of Paolo and Francesca from the *Inferno* (pp. 28–33) and of Orlando's madness from *Orlando Furioso* (pp. 70–73), all the selections are complete poems. Nearly one-third of these are sonnets, a verse form whose invention is credited to the Sicilian poet Jacopo da Lentini in the first half of the thirteenth century. Devised as a composition to be sung—the Italian word *sonetto* literally means "small sound," a brief melody—the sonnet was used by hosts of later poets in Italy and throughout Europe especially after the appearance of Petrarch's *Canzoniere*. A curious departure from the classic fourteen-line model is the tailed sonnet, which enjoyed considerable popularity during the fourteenth century and eventually came to be associated with burlesque poetry. It is really a regular sonnet, but with the added "tail" of one or more rhymed tercets. As an illustration of this variety, we have Michelangelo's ironic self-portrait "I' ho già fatto un gozzo in questo stento" ("A Giovanni da Pistoia," p. 78).

Also originally related to music was the ballad, three examples of which are offered, from Cavalcanti (p. 18), Boccaccio (p. 44), and Poliziano (p. 62). Taking its name from the verb *ballare* (to dance), the ballad was a folk song meant to be accompanied by a dance and was not used as a literary form before the second part of the thirteenth century. It consists of a two- or three-line refrain and several rhymed stanzas. The refrain was first sung by the dance leader and then repeated by the dancers in the chorus after each stanza.

Other typical verse forms represented here are the terza rima, the *caccia*, and the madrigal. The terza rima, consisting of tercets in linked rhyme (*aba–bcb–cdc*, etc.), was created by Dante (for whom the number three had a mystic significance) and is of course famous as the rhyme scheme of the *Divine Comedy*. The *caccia*, literally "hunt," a free-verse composition, was used from the fourteenth to the sixteenth centuries to describe lively scenes of hunting, fishing, marketing, love, or battle. Sacchetti's "Passando con pensier" (p. 48) is without any doubt one of the most enchanting illustrations of this genre. As for the madrigal, it was originally an improvised pastoral song. The earliest known literary madrigal was written by Petrarch. Tasso (see pp. 85–91), however, remains the unsurpassed master of this short lyric form which has no fixed metrical structure and usually expresses a poet's love for his lady.

Irrespective of the type of poem—sonnet, ballad, madrigal, terza rima, blank or free verse—by far the most common line in Italian poetry is the hendecasyllable, or eleven-syllable line. To be sure, Italian poets have made frequent use of other regular meters, particularly the septenary (seven-syllable line), but it is within the rhythm and the breadth of the hendecasyllable that Italian words seem to find their natural poetic order. As one of Italy's leading contemporary poets, Giuseppe Ungaretti, had to admit after long experimentation with irregular, purposely arhythmic, and very short lines (see "Veglia," p. 124), it is not possible to write Italian poetry and avoid the hendecasyllable, for "every true Italian poet has the hendecasyllable in his blood."

The English versions appearing in this anthology in no way attempt to be poems in their own right. They endeavor to give the closest and most faithful rendering of the Italian text in order to assist the reader in following the words of the original. Every effort has been made to translate on a line-to-line basis except where it has proved impossible because of the particular word order of the Italian. In such cases a small letter at the beginning of a line indicates that the words in that line do not all come from the corresponding single line of the Italian, but are linked to the preceding or following line, or lines (see for example the translations of Foscolo's "Alla sera," p. 99, and of Leopardi's "L' infinito," p. 105). Finally, as the reader may note, the punctuation in the translations departs at times from that of the Italian for reasons of clarity.

I should like to acknowledge with deep gratitude my indebtedness to Stanley Burnshaw, the poet and editor of *The Poem Itself*, for his advice and encouragement and in particular for his invaluable assistance in solving problems of interpretation and translation.

INTRODUCTION TO
ITALIAN POETRY

SAN FRANCESCO D'ASSISI

(c. 1182–1226)

TO people the world over Saint Francis is known as the founder of a famous religious order and a symbol of humility and brotherly love. Less known is the fact that this man, who in his early twenties severed all ties with his family and renounced wealth and social position to lead a life of poverty and meditation, is also the author of one of the first works of artistic value in Italian literature, the "Cantico delle creature."

"Cantico delle creature," Saint Francis' only work in verse form and in the vernacular (all his other writings are in Latin prose), is a sort of psalm in praise of God and His creation and vividly captures the essence of the Saint's elemental philosophy. Apart from its message, however, this poem offers a striking example of pure lyric achievement. The impact of its freshness and serene solemnity, particularly in the last stanza, where death is evoked, has not lost any of its force through the centuries. Nor are archaic and Umbrian dialect forms a serious hindrance to a modern reader for full enjoyment of the poem. It will be sufficient to remember that "so" stands for "sono," "omne" and "onne" for "ogni," "ene" for "è," "ellu" for "egli," "sostengo" for "sostengono," "ca" for "perchè," "sirano" for "saranno."

According to the oldest Franciscan sources, the "Cantico" was composed in the church of San Damiano near Assisi in 1224, the year in which Saint Francis received the stigmata. The first seven stanzas were written after a vision of eternal bliss; the eighth stanza was added some time later; and the poem was completed shortly before the Saint's death.

Cantico delle creature

Altissimu, omnipotente, bon Signore
Tue so le laude la gloria e l'honore
Et omne benedictione.
Ad te solo, Altissimo, se confano
Et nullu homo ene dignu te mentovare.

Laudato sie, mi Signore, cun tutte le tue creature
Spetialmente messor lo frate sole
Lo qual jorna et allumini noi per loi.
Et ellu è bellu e radiante cun grande splendore:
De te, Altissimo, porta significatione.

Laudato si', mi Signore, per sora luna e le stelle;
In cielo l'hai formate clarite et pretiose et belle.

Laudato si', mi Signore, per frate vento
E per aere et nubilo et sereno et onne tempo,
Per lo quale a le tue creature dai sustentamento.

Laudato si', mi Signore, per sor'acqua,
La quale è multo utile et humile et pretiosa et casta.

Laudato si', mi Signore, per frate focu
Per lo quale ennallumini la nocte;
Et ello è bello et jocundo et robustoso et forte.

Laudato si', mi Signore, per sora nostra matre terra,
La quale ne sustenta et governa,
Et produce diversi fructi con coloriti fiori et herba.

Laudato si', mi Signore, per quelli che perdonano per
    lo tuo amore
Et sostengo infirmitate et tribulatione:
Beati quelli che sosterranno in pace,
Ca da te, Altissimo, sirano incoronati.

Canticle of Living Creatures

Highest, omnipotent, good Lord,
Yours are the praises, the glory, and the honor
And every blessing.
To You alone, Most High, do they belong
And no man is worthy to speak Your name.

Praised be You, my Lord, with all Your creatures,
Especially our brother, Master Sun,
Who makes day and through whom You give us light.
And he is beautiful and radiant with great splendor:
He brings meaning of You, O Most High.

Praised be You, my Lord, for sister moon and the stars;
In heaven You have made them bright and precious and
beautiful.

Praised be You, my Lord, for brother wind
And for the air, and for cloudy and clear and for all weather,
Through which You give sustenance to Your creatures.

Praised be You, my Lord, for sister water,
Who is most useful and humble and precious and chaste.

Praised be You, my Lord, for brother fire
Through whom you illumine the night;
And he is beautiful and gay and vigorous and strong.

Praised be You, my Lord, for our sister, mother earth,
Who sustains and governs us,
And produces various fruits with colored flowers and grass.

Praised be You, my Lord, for those who forgive out of love
for You
And bear infirmity and tribulation:
Blessed are those who suffer in peace,
For by You, Most High, they shall be crowned.

Laudato si', mi Signore, per sora nostra morte corporale,
Da la quale nullu homo vivente po scappare:
Guai a quelli che morranno ne le peccata mortali,
Beati quelli che trovarà ne le tue sanctissime voluntati,
Ca la morte secunda nol farrà male.

Laudate et benedicete mi Signore et rengratiate
Et serviteli cun grande humilitate.

Praised be You, my Lord, for our sister, bodily death,
From whom no living man can escape:
Woe to those who die in mortal sin,
Blessed are those whom she will find in Your most holy will,
For the second death will do them no harm.

Praise and bless my Lord and thank Him
And serve Him with great humility.

LA COMPIUTA DONZELLA

(second half of the thirteenth century)

VERY little is known of La Compiuta Donzella, except that she was a delicate, intense poet who was born and lived in Florence—the first woman poet of marked talent to write in a modern European language. It is not even certain that Compiuta Donzella was her real name; it may have been a pseudonym meaning the Accomplished Maid. She was also referred to as the Divine Sibyl.

Only three sonnets attributed to La Compiuta Donzella are extant. They suggest that her life was torn between her desire to become a nun, perhaps the aftermath of an unhappy love affair, and her father's insistence that she marry the man of his choice. This theme is treated with moving simplicity and consummate poetic skill in "A la stagion che il mondo foglia e fiora," a sonnet that can at first be mistaken for a song in praise of spring and love. Not until the eighth line does one realize that sorrow, not joy has inspired this poem.

The limpid style of this poet and the melodiousness of her lines reveal the high degree of refinement and precision that the language of lyric poetry had attained in Tuscany in the thirteenth century. At the same time the sonnet, devised only a few decades earlier by the Sicilian Jacopo da Lentini, appears to have developed already into the perfect poetic form that before long would be imitated throughout Europe.

"A la stagion che il mondo foglia e fiora"

A la stagion che il mondo foglia e fiora,
Accresce gioia a tutti i fini amanti,
Vanno insieme a li giardini allora
Che gli augelletti fanno dolci canti,
La franca gente tutta s'innamora,
Ed in servir ciascun traggesi innanti,
Ed ogni damigella in gioi' dimora.
A me n'abbondan marrimenti e pianti.

Chè lo mio padre m'ha messa in errore,
E tienemi sovente in forte doglia:
Donar mi vuole, a mia forza, segnore.
Ed io di ciò non ho disio nè voglia,
E in gran tormento vivo a tutte l'ore:
Però non mi rallegra fior nè foglia.

"In the season when the world leafs and flowers"

In the season when the world leafs and flowers,
Joy grows in all gentle lovers,
They go together to the gardens, while
Little birds make sweet song,
All free-hearted people fall in love,
And every man steps forth to serve,
And every maiden lives in joy.
As for me, miseries and tears abound.

For my father has put me in a quandary,
And keeps me often in terrible pain:
He wants to give me—forcing me—a husband.
And I have neither wish nor will for this,
And in great torment I live every hour:
So that neither flower nor leaf rejoices me.

V gualmente finita qsto inplicami
L un con prudença Laltro follacrandola

Cançone diguido caualcanti

O Onna · mipriega · prhio uogho dire
D uno accidente · chesouente · feco
E t esi altero · cherhiamato amore
S i chi Lonega · possa · duer · sentire
D ndio alpresente conoscendo · choro
P er chio non spero · chom dibasso core
A tal ragion poeti · conoscença
C he sança natural dimostrameto ·
N ono talento · diuoler prouare
L adoue possa errhi losa · creare
E t qual sia · sua · uerti et sua · potença
L essença et poi rasnino suo mouimeto ·
E t piacimento · chelsa · dire amore
E t se huom puede Lo puo mostrare

I n quella pate doue sta · memoria
P rende suo stato · siformato came
D ya son dalume duna oscoritate
L aqual damarte uien et fa dismota
E ll e creata · chassensato nome
D alma costume et dicor uoluntate
V ien daueduta forma che sintende
C he prende nelpossibile intelletto ·
C ome insubgierto loco edimorança
I nquella parte mai nona possança ·
P er che da qualitate · non discende
R isplende inse · perpetuale effetto ·
N onna diletto · ma con sideranga
S irrhe non puote Langir simiglianga

N one uertute ma · da · qaella uiene ·

GUIDO CAVALCANTI

(c. 1260–1300)

GUIDO CAVALCANTI, one of Dante's closest friends, was the Florentine leader of the *dolce stil nuovo*, the school of poetry founded in Bologna by the other famous Guido of the thirteenth century, the jurist Guido Guinizelli. The poets of the *dolce stil nuovo*—the expression comes from Dante's *Purgatorio* and means literally the "sweet new style"—dedicated themselves to the exaltation and glorification of woman. This was by no means an original approach, having been central to Provençal poetry, but Guinizelli and his followers renovated it with a strictly philosophical emphasis based on the belief that love can be born only in "gentle hearts"—hearts noble and virtuous by nature—and that woman is an angel placed on earth for man's salvation. Love for a woman is therefore, in a sense, love for God himself. This theological doctrine of love, codified by Guinizelli in his canzone "Al cor gentil ripara sempre amore," influenced many poets, including Dante. All too often, however, the *dolce stil nuovo* writers were more concerned with philosophy than poetry and, as a result, many of their poems seem to us artificial and rhetorical, mere patterns of abstract convictions.

Cavalcanti too placed philosophy above poetry, to the extent that some of his poems, such as "Donna mi prega per ch'io voglio dire," on the nature of love, were quoted by contemporaries as philosophical treatises. Today these poems are all but forgotten. That part of Cavalcanti's work which has endured and established him as the first great Italian lyric poet consists of a few songs, ballads, and sonnets in which he set aside fixed patterns and complex abstractions and gave free rein to purely personal feelings. Such is the exquisite ballad "In un boschetto trova' pasturella," about a shepherdess encountered in the woods. The fact that Cavalcanti celebrates not a lady of high station but a country girl is in itself atypical of the *dolce stil nuovo*. Candor and directness of feeling make this little shepherdess unforgettable.

During the last part of his life, Cavalcanti, a White Guelf,

In un boschetto trova' pasturella

In un boschetto trova' pasturella
Più che la stella — bella al mi' parere.

Cavelli avea biondetti e ricciutelli
E gli occhi pien d'amor, cera rosata;
Con sua verghetta pasturav' agnelli,
E, scalza, di rugiada era bagnata;
Cantava come fosse 'nnamorata;
Er'adornata — di tutto piacere.

D'amor la salutai immantenente
E domandai s'avesse compagnia,
Ed ella mi rispuose dolcemente
Che sola sola per lo bosco gía,
E disse: "Sacci, quando l'augel pia,
Allor disia — 'l me' cor drudo avere."

Poi che mi disse di sua condizione,
E per lo bosco augelli audìo cantare,
Fra me stesso diss'io: "Or' è stagione
Di questa pasturella gioi' pigliare."
Merzè le chiesi sol che di baciare
E d'abbracciare — le fosse 'n volere.

Per man mi prese, d'amorosa voglia,
E disse che donato m'avea 'l core:
Menommi sott'una freschetta foglia
Là dov' i' vidi fior d'ogni colore,
E tanto vi sentìo gioia e dolzore
Che dio d'amore — parvemi vedere.

played a very active—even militant—role in the political life of Florence. In June 1300, after a bloody riot fomented by the rival factions of the Whites and the Blacks, he was banished with other leaders by order of the city's board of governors, among whom was Dante himself. Cavalcanti's exile lasted only a few weeks, however. Having contracted malaria, he was allowed to return to Florence, where he died in August of the same year.

In a small grove I met a little shepherdess

In a small grove I met a little shepherdess
More beautiful than the stars — she seemed to me.

She had light-blond, curly hair
And eyes full of love, rosy complexion;
With her little staff she tended lambs,
And, barefoot, she was wet with dew;
She was singing as though in love;
And she was adorned — with every delight.

I greeted her at once with love
And asked if she had any companions,
And she answered me sweetly
That she was going through the wood quite alone,
And said: "You know, when a bird calls,
Then my heart — yearns to have a lover."

After she had told me of her state,
And I had heard birds singing in the wood,
I said to myself: "Now is the time
To take pleasure in this little shepherdess."
I asked of her only permission to kiss
And to embrace — should she so wish.

She took me by the hand, with amorous desire,
And said she had given me her heart:
She led me beneath branches of cool leaves
Where I saw flowers of every color,
And there I felt such joy and sweetness
That the god of love — I seemed to see.

Soneto ritornello

22 Siofose fuocho io ardere lomondo
    sifosi uento iol tenpostarei
    sifosi mare iolalagherei
    sifosi idio lomandarei improfondo
    sifosi papa alor farei gracihondo
    chetutti icristian tribolarei
    sifosi inperadore belou farei
    atuta giente tagliare irchapo atondo

    Siofosi morte ionadre amio padre
    siofosi uita nonistarei cholui
    esimilmente farei dimia madre
    sifosi uocho chome so chefui
    noue perme legiouane legiadre
    tebeute uochie lasciarei altrui

    Venete

CECCO ANGIOLIERI

(c. 1260–1312)

IRREVERENT, sensual, deliberately vulgar and blasphemous, Cecco Angiolieri is the *enfant terrible* of the thirteenth century. The fact that his sonnets (some 150 of which are extant) could find an audience when the *dolce stil nuovo* was at its height is a measure of the sophistication of the period in which he lived.

Cecco Angiolieri was born in Siena and lived for some time in Rome. Aside from what he tells of himself in his writings, in which he draws the portrait of a dissolute man, not much is known about him. Throughout his life, he cynically proclaimed in one poem, only three things interested him: women, the tavern, and dice. But to obtain all three, he needed money— which he never possessed in sufficient amounts. Money and the impossible character of Becchina, a leather worker's daughter with whom he was in love, seem to have been the chief problems of his existence. He was a person who apparently had no fear or respect for any one: God, the Pope, his parents, his contemporaries. For example, in a sarcastic sonnet he referred to Dante as an "ox."

All the irascibility and fury of this angry man of the Middle Ages would of course be of no importance if he had not also been a powerful and original artist. Indeed, Angiolieri's singular gifts as an epigrammatic, satiric poet, his verbal boldness, his irony, his sense of the comic and the grotesque make him a master of this genre. In his most famous poem, "S'i' fosse foco, arderei 'l mondo," he superbly conveys within the fourteen lines of a sonnet his hatred for the world together with his lust for living.

"S'i' fosse foco, arderei 'l mondo"

S'i' fosse foco, arderei 'l mondo;
S'i' fosse vento, lo tempesterei;
S'i' fosse acqua, i' l'annegherei;
S'i' fosse Dio, mandereil' in profondo.
S'i' fosse papa, sare' allor giocondo,
Che tutt'i cristiani imbrigherei;
S'i' fosse 'mperator, sa' che farei?
A tutti mozzarei lo capo a tondo.

S'i' fosse morte, andarei da mio padre;
S'i' fosse vita, fuggirei da lui;
Similmente faria da mi' madre.
S'i' fosse Cecco, com'i' sono e fui,
Torrei le donne giovani e leggiadre,
E vecchie e laide lasserei altrui.

"If I were fire, I would set the world aflame"

If I were fire, I would set the world aflame;
If I were wind, I would storm it;
If I were water, I would drown it;
If I were God, I would send it to the abyss.
If I were Pope, then I would be happy,
For I would swindle all the Christians;
If I were Emperor, do you know what I would do?
I would chop off heads all around.

If I were death, I would go to my father;
If I were life, I would flee from him;
The same I would do with my mother.
If I were Cecco, as I am and I was,
I would take the women who are young and lovely,
And leave the old and ugly for others.

DANTE ALIGHIERI

(1265–1321)

IN a page of his *Comedy* (the adjective "divine" was added later by Boccaccio), Dante gave this definition of himself:

> . . . Io mi son un che, quando
> Amor mi spira. noto, ed a quel modo
> Ch'ei detta dentro, vo significando.

[. . . I am one who takes note when inspired by love, and in the very way that it dictates within me, so I go shedding meaning.]

Dante was nine years old when he first saw Beatrice Portinari, who was a few months younger than he and lived close to his home in Florence. From that moment, he wrote, "love ruled my soul." Beatrice was to marry Simone de' Bardi, a wealthy banker, and it is improbable that she ever knew of Dante's admiration for her. As for Dante, he married Gemma Donati, by whom he had four children, and certainly was attracted to other women. Nevertheless, it was his platonic love for Beatrice—"the woman of my mind," as he described her—which was to be the inspiration of his life and work. After her death in 1290 at the age of twenty-five, Dante composed the *Vita nova*, a collection of poems interlaced with a prose commentary, in which he told the story of his ideal love. Most famous of these poems is the sonnet "Tanto gentile e tanto onesta pare," given below, a fine example of *dolce stil nuovo* poetry. Beatrice is portrayed not as a human being but as an angel whose presence on earth is a miracle. The love she inspires is a spiritual bliss, one conveyed to a man's heart through his eyes, excluding even the remotest implication of physical contact.

Unlike Beatrice, Francesca da Rimini, the protagonist of our second selection, from the *Divine Comedy*, is a woman in a wholly terrestrial sense. She too is endowed with attributes exalted by the poets of the *dolce stil nuovo*—gentleness, purity of heart, courtesy, and modesty of demeanor. But she also has the weakness and fragility of a woman whom love overwhelms and leads into sin. Francesca's tragic passion for her brother-in-law ended with the murder of the two lovers surprised in adultery by the husband. The story was of course well known to Dante, who spent several years in Francesca's native city, Ravenna, after his banishment from Florence in 1302 for political reasons.

Dante placed Francesca in the second circle of hell with the carnal sinners condemned to be buffeted eternally by a violent wind, symbolic of the lustful passion to which they had succumbed. The thought of the sin she committed and her resulting damnation is ever present in Francesca's account of her love for Paolo, yet the portrait Dante draws of her is not merely that of a sinner. Nor does he add to God's condemnation his own, as is often the case in the *Inferno*. On the contrary, his attitude is one of compassion and pity, even of sympathy. So that it is plausible to assume that with Francesca, the tragic victim of an overpowering yearning of the senses, Dante identified himself, thinking of the love affairs which in his youth had led him away from the platonic ideal of purity and perfection personified by Beatrice. He himself, in the opening lines of the *Divine Comedy*, referred to this period of his existence through the metaphor of the "selva oscura," the dark forest of sin in which he had become entangled, losing his way. Dante was saved by Beatrice, who appealed to God on his behalf. Francesca da Rimini was denied the opportunity to repent, having been murdered when she was in a state of mortal sin. Her punishment was the unrelenting memory of her love for Paolo, a love which continued to inflame her in hell with the same power it had possessed on earth—a reminder, sweet and terrible, of the irrevocability of her fate.

It is of course impossible to deal adequately in a few paragraphs with a figure so rich and complex as Dante. The *Divine Comedy*, whose declared aim was "to remove those who live on this earth from their state of misery and lead them into a state of happiness," besides being a masterpiece of poetry, is a powerful structure of medieval philosophy and doctrine which must be grasped in its unity of thought and design before one can fully appreciate the single parts and episodes that compose it. Nevertheless, even by themselves, the Beatrice sonnet in the *Vita nova* and the Francesca canto in the *Inferno*, in the diversity of tone and inspiration, are excellent introductions to Dante's two major works and admirable examples of his art.

"*Tanto gentile e tanto onesta pare*"

Tanto gentile e tanto onesta pare
La donna mia quand'ella altrui saluta
Ch'ogne lingua deven tremando muta,
E li occhi no l'ardiscon di guardare.
Ella si va, sentendosi laudare,
Benignamente d'umiltà vestuta;
E par che sia una cosa venuta
Da cielo in terra a miracol mostrare.

Mostrasi sì piacente a chi la mira,
Che dà per li occhi una dolcezza al core,
Che 'ntender no la può chi no la prova;
E par che de la sua labbia si mova
Un spirito soave pien d'amore,
Che va dicendo a l'anima: "Sospira."

Francesca da Rimini (Inferno, *dal Canto V°*)

Io cominciai: "Poeta, volentieri
Parlerei a que' due che insieme vanno,
E paion sì al vento esser leggieri."
Ed egli a me: "Vedrai, quando saranno
Più presso a noi; e tu allor li prega
Per quell'amor che i mena: ed ei verranno."
Sì tosto come il vento a noi li piega,
Mossi la voce: "O anime affannate,
Venite a noi parlar, s'altri nol niega!"
Quali colombe dal disio chiamate,

"So gentle and so virtuous she appears"

So gentle and so virtuous she appears,
My lady, when greeting other people
That every tongue tremblingly grows silent,
And eyes do not dare gaze upon her.
She passes by, hearing herself praised,
Graciously clothed with humility,
And she appears to be a creature who has come
From heaven to earth to show forth a miracle.

She shows herself so pleasing to her beholders,
That she gives through the eyes a sweetness to the heart,
Which no one can understand who does not feel it;
And it appears that from her lip moves
A tender spirit full of love,
Which says again and again to the soul: "Sigh."

Francesca da Rimini (*Inferno*, from Canto V)

I began: "O poet,[1] willingly
Would I speak to those two who go as one,
And seem to be so light in the wind."
And he to me: "You shall see, when they are
Closer to us; and then address them
In the name of that love which drives them, and they will
*   come."*
As soon as the wind bent them towards us,
I moved my voice: "O anguished souls,
Come and speak to us, if no one forbids it!"
As doves called by desire,

---

[1] Virgil, Dante's mentor and guide.

Con l'ali alzate e ferme al dolce nido
Volan per l'aere dal voler portate;
Cotali uscir dalla schiera ov'è Dido,
A noi venendo per l'aer maligno,
Sì forte fu l'affettuoso grido.
"O animal grazioso e benigno,
Che visitando vai per l'aer perso
Noi che tignemmo il mondo di sanguigno,
Se fosse amico il re dell'universo
Noi pregheremmo lui per la tua pace,
Poi che hai pietà del nostro mal perverso.
Di quel che udire e che parlar ti piace,
Noi udiremo e parleremo a vui,
Mentre che il vento, come fa, si tace.
Siede la terra dove nata fui,
Su la marina dove il Po discende
Per aver pace co' seguaci sui.
Amor, che al cor gentil ratto s'apprende,
Prese costui della bella persona
Che mi fu tolta; e il modo ancor m'offende.
Amor, che a nullo amato amar perdona,
Mi prese del costui piacer sì forte,
Che, come vedi, ancor non m'abbandona.
Amor condusse noi ad una morte:
Caina attende chi a vita ci spense."
Queste parole da lor ci fur porte.
Da che io intesi quelle anime offense,
Chinai il viso, e tanto il tenni basso,
Fin che il poeta mi disse: "Che pense?"
Quando risposi, cominciai: "Oh lasso,
Quanti dolci pensier, quanto disio
Menò costoro al doloroso passo!"
Poi mi rivolsi a loro e parla' io,

With raised, motionless wings to their sweet nest
Glide through the air, borne by their will;
So they departed from the band where Dido[2] is,
And came to us through the malignant air,
So powerful was my affectionate cry.
"O creature full of grace and kind
Who walk through this dark air to visit
Us who stained the earth blood-red,
If the king of the universe were our friend
We would beg of him peace for you,
For you have pity on our perverse evil.
Of that which it pleases you to hear and to speak
We shall hear and we shall speak with you,
While the wind is silent, as it is now.
The land where I was born sits
On the seashore where the Po goes down
To find peace with its companion rivers.
Love, which swifty takes hold of a gentle heart,
Captured this one with the beautiful body
Which was taken from me; and the manner still offends me.
Love, which pardons no loved one for not loving,
Captured me with this one's charm so securely
That, as you see, it still does not leave me.
Love led us to one death:
Caina[3] awaits him who snuffed out our lives."
These words were offered us by them.
After I listened to those offended souls,
I bent my head, and held it very low,
Until the poet said: "What are you thinking?"
When I replied, I began: "Alas,
How many sweet thoughts, how much desire
Led those two to their dolorous pass!"
Then I turned to them and it was I who spoke,

[2] Dido, Queen of Carthage, is one of the carnal sinners of the second circle of hell.

[3] A section of the deepest part of hell, where betrayers of their own kindred expiate their sins.

E cominciai: "Francesca, i tuoi martiri
A lagrimar mi fanno tristo e pio.
Ma dimmi: al tempo de' dolci sospiri,
A che e come concedette amore
Che conosceste i dubbiosi desiri?"
Ed ella a me: "Nessun maggior dolore
Che ricordarsi del tempo felice
Nella miseria: e ciò sa il tuo dottore.
Ma se a conoscer la prima radice
Del nostro amor tu hai cotanto affetto,
Farò come colui che piange e dice.
Noi leggevamo un giorno per diletto
Di Lancialotto, come amor lo strinse;
Soli eravamo e senza alcun sospetto.
Per più fiate gli occhi ci sospinse
Quella lettura, e scolorocci il viso;
Ma solo un punto fu quel che ci vinse.
Quando leggemmo il disiato riso
Esser baciato da cotanto amante,
Questi, che mai da me non fia diviso,
La bocca mi baciò tutto tremante.
Galeotto fu il libro e chi lo scrisse:
Quel giorno più non vi leggemmo avante."
Mentre che l'uno spirto questo disse,
L'altro piangeva sì, che di pietade
Io venni men così com'io morisse;
E caddi, come corpo morto cade.

And I began: "Francesca, your martyrdoms
Make me shed tears, sad and full of pity.
But tell me: at the time of the sweet sighs,
How, by what means did Love allow you
To know each other's dubious desires?"
And she to me: "There is no greater pain
Than to remember a happy time
In misery; and this your mentor knows.
But if for understanding the first root
Of our love you have such tender feeling,
I shall do as one who weeps and speaks.
We were reading one day for our pleasure
Of Lancelot, how love clasped him;
We were alone, and without any suspicion.
Many times were our eyes drawn together
By that reading, and color drained from our faces;
But one point only was there which vanquished us.
When we read of how her[4] desired smile
Was kissed by such a lover,
This one, who never will be parted from me,
Kissed my mouth all trembling.
Gallehault[5] was the book and he who wrote it:
That day we read in it no farther."
While thus one spirit spoke,
The other one so wept, that from pitying
I grew faint as if dying;
And I fell as a dead body falls.

[4] The lady referred to here is of course Guinevere.
[5] The intermediary who brought Lancelot and Guinevere together.

FRANCESCO PETRARCA

(1304–1374)

THE span of scarcely more than one generation separates
Dante and Petrarch. Yet between the *Divine Comedy* and the
Canzoniere there is a profound difference of tone and sensitivity;
the two masterpieces seem to belong to epochs far distant one
from the other. One might say that the Middle Ages, with their
essentially mystical and ethical conception of life based on the
dogmas of Christian faith, ended with Dante, and that with
Petrarch a new era opened—distinctive for its love of nature and
earthly pleasures, its quest for happiness in this world, its doubts
and contradictions.

Petrarch, like Dante, was a believer: in the religious values of
life, in the necessity to ensure the salvation of the soul and to
resist the temptations of the flesh. But in practice he leaned to-
ward a brilliant, mundane life; and his refined taste, cultivated on
the Latin and Greek classics, brought him to regard the Middle
Ages as a time of obscurantism and barbarity. Dante himself was
not highly esteemed by Petrarch, who preferred authors of the
pre-Christian, pagan world: Cicero, Livy, Horace, Virgil, Homer.
Besides, he was deeply convinced that posterity would remember
him for his Latin verse, for which he had been honored in his
thirty-seventh year with a coronation ceremony on the Capitoline
Hill in Rome. Petrarch always affected great scorn for his love
poems written in Italian, and only in the last years of his life did
he decide to arrange them in a volume to which he gave a Latin
title: *Rerum Vulgarium Fragmenta*. Yet it is for the *Canzoniere*, as
later generations rebaptized his splendid lyric "fragments" (and

to a lesser extent for his other work in Italian—*Trionfi*, Triumphs
—an allegorical poem in terza rima probably written in an
attempt to emulate the *Divine Comedy*), that Petrarch was ad-
mired throughout Europe and imitated in the form of a new liter-
ary genre, Petrarchism.

The *Canzoniere* is dedicated to Laura, whom the poet met in
Avignon, where his father, a lawyer, had settled with the retinue
of the papal court. Laura's exact identity has been the subject of
long debate. It seems that her name was Laure de Noves, that
she was the wife of the nobleman Hugo de Sade, to whom she
bore eleven children, that she had been married two years when
Petrarch first saw her, on Good Friday, 1327. She died twenty-one
years later during an epidemic of the plague. Laura never re-
turned Petrarch's sentiments, and for his part the poet always
professed to see in her only a Platonic ideal of perfection and
purity. It is difficult, however, to reconcile this assertion with the

"*Solo e pensoso i più deserti campi*"

Solo e pensoso i più deserti campi
Vo mesurando a passi tardi e lenti,
E gli occhi porto per fuggire intenti
Ove vestigio uman l'arena stampi.
Altro schermo non trovo che mi scampi
Dal manifesto accorger de le genti,
Perchè negli atti d'allegrezza spenti
Di fuor si legge com'io dentro avampi:

Sì ch'io mi credo omai che monti e piagge
E fiumi e selve sappian di che tempre
Sia la mia vita, ch'è celata altrui.
Ma pur sì aspre vie nè sì selvagge
Cercar non so, ch'Amor non venga sempre
Ragionando con meco, ed io con lui.

frequently sensual tone he used in describing her physical beauty.

For Petrarch, Laura was a source of both delight and torment; she bound him to material things despite himself, awakened desires and temptations, and turned his mind from God. In the most dramatic moments of his monologue Petrarch considered his devotion to Laura shameful and sinful. The sonnets here included describe his surrender to a passion which he felt powerless to overcome. He knew that his obsessive attachment to Laura imperiled his salvation, yet he could find peace only in thinking of her. Petrarch could not resolve his inner conflict so long as Laura was alive. But his gift for observing and recording his own contradictory feelings and spiritual anxieties helped him to create in the *Canzoniere* not only poetry of unsurpassed beauty but also a model of psychological analysis whose impact is still felt in our day.

"Alone and pensive, the most deserted fields"

Alone and pensive, the most deserted fields
I pace with steps lagging and slow,
And I hold my eyes watchfully, so as to flee
Wherever human traces mark the sand.
I find no other screen to protect me
From people's manifest awareness [of my state],
For in my acts extinct of joy
They can read from without how inwardly I blaze:

So that I now believe mountains and shores
And rivers and forests know of what temper
My life is, hidden from others.
And yet pathways so rough or wild
I know not how to seek where Love would not always come
Reasoning with me, and I with him.

"Or che 'l ciel e la terra e l' vento tace"

Or che 'l ciel e la terra e 'l vento tace,
E le fere e gli augelli il sonno affrena,
Notte il carro stellato in giro mena,
E nel suo letto il mar senz'onda giace;
Vegghio, penso, ardo, piango; e chi mi sface
Sempre m'è innanzi per mia dolce pena:
Guerra è il mio stato, d'ira e di duol piena;
E sol di lei pensando ho qualche pace.

Così sol d'una chiara fonte viva
Move 'l dolce e l'amaro ond'io mi pasco;
Una man sola mi risana e punge.
E perchè 'l mio martir non giunga a riva,
Mille volte il dì moro e mille nasco;
Tanto dalla salute mia son lunge.

"Now that the sky and earth and wind are still"

Now that the sky and earth and wind are still,
And beasts and birds are stayed by sleep,
Night leads her starry chariot on its round,
And without waves the sea lies in its bed;
I am awake, I think, I burn, I weep; and she who is my
*   undoing*
Is ever before me to my sweet pain:
War is my state, full of wrath and grief;
And only in thinking of her do I have some peace.

Thus from the same clear living spring
Flow the sweet and the bitter on which I feed;
One hand alone heals me and stabs me.
And so that my martyrdom may not reach the shore,
A thousand times a day I die and a thousand I am born;
So far away am I from my salvation.

GIOVANNI BOCCACCIO

(1313–1375)

GIOVANNI BOCCACCIO, the third of the Tuscan literary giants of the fourteenth century, was a life-long admirer of Dante and Petrarch as well as an intimate friend of the latter. He was drawn to the study of their works (his writings include a commentary on the first seventeen cantos of the *Divine Comedy*) by his precocious love for poetry: "I had not yet reached my seventh year, and I had not read verse or listened to any master, when, moved by nature itself, I felt a desire for poetry."

Boccaccio composed several poetical works, among them: *Filostrato* (The Man Overcome by Love), *Teseida* (The Tale of Theseus), epic romances which Chaucer admired and imitated, *Ninfale fiesolano* (The Nymph of Fiesole), a mythological-pastoral idyll generally acknowledged to be the best of his minor works, and a collection of *Rime* (Rhymes), whose prevalent theme is the poet's passion for a lady he calls Fiammetta. She was, some believe, Maria d'Aquino, natural daughter of Robert, King of Anjou, whose splendid and corrupt court in Naples Boccaccio frequented during his stay in that city between 1328 and 1340. The story goes that Fiammetta, after spurning Boccaccio's suit, finally surrendered only to leave him inconsolable when she later betrayed him. Several critics, however, have questioned the probability of this love affair, just as they have cast doubt on the widespread belief that Boccaccio was born in Paris, the illegitimate son of a French noblewoman, Jeanne (hence the name Giovanni given the child) de la Roche. The fact remains that Fiammetta, real or imaginary, plays the same source-of-inspiration role in

Boccaccio's work as Beatrice in Dante's and Laura in Petrarch's, and this despite the profound differences between Boccaccio's personality and those of his famous predecessors. For Boccaccio excelled in narrative prose rather than poetry and his lyric production, however rich in quantity, remains of secondary importance.

Most of Boccaccio's "Rhymes" are marred by excessive erudition and a too obvious attempt to imitate Dante and Petrarch. There are a few poems, however, which do succeed in achieving lyric originality and remarkable freshness of movement. Among these, characteristically, are the ballads which conclude each of the ten "days" of his masterpiece, the collection of one hundred short stories to which he gave the Greek-derived title of *Decameron*. Boccaccio imagined that in the year 1348, while Florence was ravaged by the plague, seven ladies met by chance with three young gentlemen in the church of Santa Maria Novella, and on the spot decided to flee the pestilence together, for they said,

"It is natural for anybody who is alive to protect, preserve, and defend his life." They took shelter in a villa on the hills overlooking the city and there, oblivious to the suffering and death of their compatriots, they resided for ten days, whiling away the time in pleasant occupations. Every afternoon, for instance, each of the ten would tell a story to entertain the company (thus totaling one hundred novellas over the ten-day period), and at night, one of the ladies would sing a ballad of love.

Our selection, the ballad which concludes the Ninth Day of the *Decameron*, is probably the best poem written by Boccaccio, full of grace and agile rhythm, and delicately sensual. This ballad also exemplifies Boccaccio's view of pleasure, so fundamental to an understanding of his realistic approach to life and love. Note the woman's complete submission to her lover, a reversal of *dolce stil nuovo* philosophy, and the use of the words "flowers" and "pleasures," played interchangeably and in deliberately ambiguous constructions.

"Io mi son giovinetta, e volentieri"

Io mi son giovinetta, e volentieri
M'allegro e canto en la stagion novella,
Merzè d'Amore e de' dolci pensieri.

Io vo pe' verdi prati riguardando
I bianchi fiori e gialli e i vermigli,
Le rose in su le spine e i bianchi gigli,
E tutti quanti gli vo somigliando
Al viso di colui che me, amando,
Ha presa e terrà sempre, come quella
Ch'altro non ha in disio ch'e suoi piaceri.

De' quai quand'io ne truovo alcun che sia,
Al mio parer, ben simile di lui,
Il colgo e bacio, e parlomi con lui,
E com'io so, così l'anima mia
Tututta gli apro, e ciò che 'l cor disia:
Quindi con altri il metto in ghirlandella,
Legato co' miei crin biondi e leggeri.

E quel piacer che di natura il fiore
Agli occhi porge, quel simil mel dona
Che s'io vedessi la propria persona
Che m'ha accesa del suo dolce amore;
Quel che mi faccia più il suo odore,
Esprimer nol potrei con la favella,
Ma i sospir ne son testimon veri.

Li quai non escon già mai del mio petto,
Come dell'altre donne, aspri nè gravi,
Ma se ne vengon fuor caldi e soavi,
Et al mio amor sen vanno nel cospetto;
Il qual, come gli sente, a dar diletto
Di sè a me si move e viene in quella
Ch'i' son per dir: "Deh vien', ch'i' non disperi."

"I am a young maiden, and I willingly"

I am a young maiden, and I willingly
Rejoice and sing in the new season,
Thanks to love and to my sweet thoughts.

I wander through green meadows gazing
At the white and yellow and vermilion flowers,
At the roses above their thorns and the white lilies,
And all of them I liken
To the face of him who, loving me,
Took me and forever will keep me as the one
Who desires nothing but his pleasures.

Among these when I find one which is,
In my view, very much like him,
I pluck it and kiss it and talk with it,
And as best I can, thus my soul
I open entirely to it, and [also] my heart's desires:
Then I place it in a garland with others
Tied with my light, blond hair.

And that pleasure which nature's flower
Offers the eyes—a similar one it gives me
As though I were seeing the very person
Who has inflamed me with his sweet love;
What else its odor does to me
I could not express in words,
But my sighs bear true witness thereof.

They never rise out of my breast,
As out of other women's, harsh or heavy,
But come forth warm and smooth,
And go to my lover's presence;
And he, feeling them, stirs to give me delight
of himself, and comes at that moment
When I am about to say: "Come, ah! come, lest I despair."

FRANCO SACCHETTI

(c. 1330–1400)

WITH Franco Sacchetti, the glorious Trecento, which had opened with the *Divine Comedy*, closed on something of an anticlimax. It is not known whether he was born in Florence or Dalmatia, where his father had settled. He was a merchant by profession, traveled widely in Italy and Europe, and held various public appointments in several small Tuscan towns.

Although Sacchetti belonged to an old, noble Florentine family mentioned by Dante in a canto of the *Paradiso*, his art, whether in prose or poetry (he is famous primarily for his short stories) can hardly be described as aristocratic. A man of average culture and modest ambition, Sacchetti did not write about great lovers, heroes, or pagan gods; he avoided complex ideas and philosophical arguments, content with depicting everyday situations and ordinary men and women of the middle and lower classes. He was a master, however, in capturing the spontaneity of their most natural and characteristic attitudes as well as their free, unaffected dialogues. His poetry conveys the feeling of country life with its idyllic settings, easy laughter, and broad humor.

In contrast to the lofty style of Dante and Petrarch and the erudite and refined language of Boccaccio, Sacchetti relied on matter-of-fact, familiar phraseology. Frequently he used free verse instead of hendecasyllables, and replaced complex metrical structure with simple rhythmic effects and occasional rhymes.

The poem which follows, a striking example of Sacchetti's capacity to recreate a lively woodland scene, belongs to a short-lived genre called *caccia* (literally "hunt") and was probably written, like other lyrics of its kind, to be set to music.

"Passando con pensier per un boschetto"

Passando con pensier per un boschetto,
Donne per quello givan fior cogliendo,
"To' quel, to' quel" dicendo,
"Eccolo! eccolo!"
"Che è, che è?"
"È fior alliso."
"Va' là per le viole!"
"Omè, chè 'l prun mi punge!"
"Quell'altra me' v'aggiunge."
"Uh! uh! o che è quel che salta?"
"È un grillo."
"Venite qua, correte:
Raponzoli cogliete."
"E' non son essi." "Sì, sono."
"Colei, o colei,
Vie' qua. Vie' qua pe' funghi."
"Costà, costà pel sermollino."
"No' starem troppo,
Chè 'l tempo si turba!"
"E' balena."
"E' truona."
"E vespero già suona."
"Non è egli ancor nona."
"Odi, odi:
È l'usignuol che canta:
Più bel v'è,
Più bel v'è."
"I' sento . . . e non so che."
"Ove?" "Dove?"

"As I was walking pensively through a little wood"

As I was walking pensively through a little
wood,
Women were there gathering flowers,
"Get that one, get that one," they were saying.
"Here it is! here it is!"
"What is it, what is it?"
"It's a lily."
"Over there, for the violets!"
"Oh my, how the thorns prick me!"
"That other [girl] gets in there better than I."
"Ooh! ooh! oh what's that jumping?"
"It's a cricket."
"Come here, hurry:
Pick some rampions."
"That's not it." "Yes, it is."
"Hey there, you there,
Come here. Come here for mushrooms."
"Stay there where you are for thyme."
"We mustn't stay too long,
For the weather's changing!"
"It's lightening."
"It's thundering."
"And vespers are chiming already."
"It's not yet three o'clock."[1]
"Listen, listen:
It's the nightingale singing:
Più bel v'è,
Più bel v'è."[2]
"I hear something . . . and I don't know what it is."
"Where?" "Oh, where?"

---

[1] Literally "Nones," or "the ninth [ecclesiastical] hour." The usual hour for vespers is five or six.

[2] Onomatopoetic words for the nightingale's song, meaning literally "More beautiful there is."

"In quel cespuglio."
Tocca, picchia, ritocca,
Mentre che 'l busso cresce,
Ed una serpe n'esce.
"Omè trista!" "Omè lassa!"
"Omè!"
Fuggendo tutte di paura piene,
Una gran piova viene.
Qual sdrucciola,
Qual cade,
Qual si punge lo pede.
A terra van ghirlande.
Tal ciò c'ha colto lascia, e tal percuote.
Tiensi beata chi più correr puote.
Sì fiso stetti il dì che lor mirai,
Ch'io non m'avidi, e tutto mi bagnai.

"In that bush."
Poke, strike, poke again,
As the uproar increases,
Out comes a snake.
"Oh, poor me!" "Oh, miserable me!"
"Oh—oh—me!"
While they all dash away full of fear,
A heavy rain comes down.
One of them slips,
Another tumbles,
A third one pricks her foot.
Garlands fall to the ground.
This one drops what she gathered, that one
        stumbles.
She who runs fastest thinks herself lucky.
So transfixed was I the day I beheld them,
That I forgot about myself, and got soaking wet.

LORENZO DE' MEDICI

(1449-1492)

STATESMAN, poet, philosopher, art patron, Lorenzo de' Medici ranks among the outstanding personalities of the Italian Renaissance. Popularly referred to as "Il Magnifico"— The Magnificent—he became the ruler of Florence at the age of twenty, remained in power for twenty-three years until his death, and brought his native city to a peak of unequaled splendor.

The young prince's munificence attracted to Florence the greatest Italian scholars, scientists, and artists of the time. Among them were Marsilio Ficino, the translator of Plato's works and the major exponent of Platonism in the Christian world; the mathematician and astronomer Toscanelli, who was the first to have presented the idea of reaching Asia by the western route and thus directly inspired Columbus; the poet and humanist Poliziano (see pp. 61–65); and painters, sculptors, architects, from Botticelli, Andrea della Robbia, Verrocchio, Pollaiuolo, and Benedetto da Maiano to Leonardo da Vinci and Michelangelo.

Lorenzo himself achieved artistic distinction as one of the foremost poets of the century. His many works are extraordinarily varied in kind and inspiration, ranging from imitations of Dante and of Petrarch to parodies of the *Divine Comedy* and of Petrarch's *Triumphs*; from religious lyrics and plays to obscene ballads; and from Platonic love poems to carnival songs. The most famous of these songs, and certainly Lorenzo's best-known single composition, is the "Triumph of Bacchus and Ariadne," included here. It is a description of a carnival procession in which living people represented mythological figures. Lorenzo was also the author of the first critical anthology of Italian lyric poetry, which he edited at the request of Frederick of Aragon, son of the King of Naples.

The versatility which Lorenzo showed throughout his writing is one of the characteristics he shared with the highly talented men at his court, but it does not fully account for the complexity of his personality and the eclecticism of his mind. Critics and historians have found it difficult to define Lorenzo's character and true nature. Machiavelli, who tried, concluded that "if one examines the light and serious side of his life, one sees in him two different persons joined with an almost impossible conjunction." Indeed, Lorenzo il Magnifico was an enigmatic man, both despotic and liberal, aristocratic and vulgar, Platonic and Epicurean, a Christian and a cynic, a realist and a romantic.

Lorenzo's greatest gift, other than his talent for poetry, was his statesmanship. He was the last Italian prince, before the advent of the House of Savoy in the nineteenth century, to exercise influence and authority over the peninsula's various cities and states, which were constantly torn by ambitions and rivalries. While he lived he was able to preserve an uneasy status quo among them, and by so doing to stave off the threat of alien intervention. But only two years after his death, the balance of power he had successfully enforced was broken. Charles VIII of France was able to invade the country virtually unchallenged, bringing the overthrow and exile of the Medicis in his wake and marking the beginning in Italy of almost four centuries of foreign domination.

Through the magical refrain of the "Triumph of Bacchus and Ariadne" and its melancholy, quasi-obsessive reminder of the rapid passing of youth and the uncertainty of tomorrow, Lorenzo perhaps was expressing the premonition that the time to enjoy life and be merry would soon be over in Florence and that sweeping historical changes could not be forestalled much longer.

Trionfo di Bacco e di Arianna

Quant'è bella giovinezza
Che si fugge tuttavia!
Chi vuol esser lieto, sia:
Di doman non c'è certezza.

Quest'è Bacco e Arianna,
Belli, e l'un dell'altro ardenti:
Perchè 'l tempo fugge e 'nganna,
Sempre insieme stan contenti.
Queste ninfe e altre genti
Sono allegre tuttavia.
Chi vuol esser lieto, sia:
Di doman non c'è certezza.

Questi lieti satiretti
Delle ninfe innamorati
Per caverne e per boschetti
Han lor posto cento agguati:
Or da Bacco riscaldati,
Ballan, saltan tuttavia.
Chi vuol esser lieto, sia:
Di doman non c'è certezza.

Queste ninfe hanno anco caro
Da loro essere ingannate;
Non puon far a Amor riparo
Se non genti rozze e 'ngrate:
Ora insieme mescolate
Suonan, cantan tuttavia.
Chi vuol esser lieto, sia:
Di doman non c'è certezza.

Triumph of Bacchus and Ariadne

How beautiful youth is
Though ever fleeing!
Let him be happy who wants to be:
There's no certainty of tomorrow.

Here are Bacchus and Ariadne,
Handsome, and burning for each other:
Because time flies and beguiles,
They remain ever happy together.
These nymphs and these others
Are always merry.
Let him be happy who wants to be:
There's no certainty of tomorrow.

These happy little satyrs
Enamored of the nymphs
In caves and groves
Have set a hundred traps for them:
Now warmed by Bacchus,
They're always dancing and leaping.
Let him be happy who wants to be:
There's no certainty of tomorrow.

These nymphs in turn are glad
To be beguiled by them;
No one can shield himself from Love
Except crude and ungrateful people:
Now mingling together
They play instruments and sing always.
Let him be happy who wants to be:
There's no certainty of tomorrow.

Questa soma che vien dreto
Sopra l'asino, è Sileno:
Così vecchio è ebbro e lieto,
Già di carne e d'anni pieno;
Se non può star ritto, almeno
Ride e gode tuttavia.
Chi vuol esser lieto, sia:
Di doman non c'è certezza.

Mida vien dopo costoro:
Ciò che tocca, oro diventa.
E che giova aver tesoro,
S'altri poi non si contenta?
Che dolcezza vuoi che senta
Chi ha sete tuttavia?
Chi vuol esser lieto, sia:
Di doman non c'è certezza.

Ciascun apra ben gli orecchi:
Di doman nessun si paschi;
Oggi siam, giovani e vecchi,
Lieti ognun, femmine e maschi;
Ogni tristo pensier caschi;
Facciam festa tuttavia.
Chi vuol esser lieto, sia:
Di doman non c'è certezza.

Donne e giovanetti amanti,
Viva Bacco e viva Amore!
Ciascun suoni, balli e canti!
Arda di dolcezza il core!
Non fatica, non dolore!
Quel c'ha esser, convien sia.
Chi vuol esser lieto, sia:
Di doman non c'è certezza.

Quant'è bella giovinezza
Che si fugge tuttavia!

This load coming behind
Upon the ass, is Silenus:
Old as he is, he's drunk and happy,
Already full of flesh and years;
If he can't hold himself straight, at least
He laughs and revels always.
Let him be happy who wants to be:
There's no certainty of tomorrow.

Midas comes after these:
Whatever he touches turns to gold.
And what's the good of having treasure,
If one then is not satisfied?
What sweet pleasure do you think he feels—
One who is always thirsty?
Let him be happy who wants to be:
There's no certainty of tomorrow.

Let every one open his ears well:
Let no one feed on tomorrow;
Today, young and old, let's be
Happy, everybody, women and men:
May every sad thought fall away;
Let's be celebrating always.
Let him be happy who wants to be:
There's no certainty of tomorrow.

Ladies and young men in love,
Long live Bacchus and long live Love!
Let every one make music, dance, and sing!
Let hearts be fired with sweetness!
No straining, no grieving!
Whatever has to be, must be.
Let him be happy who wants to be:
There's no certainty of tomorrow.

How beautiful youth is
Though ever fleeing!

ANGELO POLIZIANO

(1454–1494)

NO writer expressed better than Poliziano the ideals of the artists and of the brilliant society of men and women who during the fifteenth century gathered in such Renaissance centers as Venice and Florence, Rome and Naples, Milan and Ferrara, Mantua and Urbino. These ideals culminated in a refined, Epicurean vision of a life devoted to learning, aesthetic enjoyment, and love. Moral concerns, religion, and political philosophy, after having dominated men's thoughts during previous centuries, now aroused little or no interest. Elegance, grace, fantasy, erudition were the qualities most praised and sought after. They were blended to perfection in the verses of Angelo Poliziano.

Poliziano's family name was Ambrogini, but, characteristically, he changed it to an Italianization of Mons Politianus, the Latin name for the town of Montepulciano where he was born. A translation of the *Iliad*, undertaken when he was sixteen, brought him sudden fame and led to his introduction to Lorenzo de' Medici. The Prince, who was barely five years older than the teenage scholar, took him into his household, became his protector and friend, and entrusted him with the education of his son Piero.

Save for a short period during which Poliziano lived at the court in Mantua (he had quarreled with Lorenzo's wife and temporarily lost the Medicis' favor), he spent all his life in Florence, ultimately becoming professor of Latin and Greek at the University. His major works are the *Favola di Orfeo* (The Fable of Orpheus), the first non-religious drama in Italian literature; *Stanze per la giostra* (Stanzas for the Joust), an exquisite, though incomplete poem on the occasion of a tournament victory by Lorenzo's brother Giuliano (from this poem Botticelli drew the inspiration for his famous paintings "Spring" and "The Birth of Venus"); and a collection of ballads composed to be sung by young people dancing.

The ballad, "Ben venga maggio," which follows, is among the finest things Poliziano wrote. Its theme—the enjoyment of life

"Ben venga Maggio"

Ben venga maggio
E 'l gonfalon selvaggio:

Ben venga primavera
Che vuol l'uom s'innamori
E voi, donzelle, a schiera
Con li vostri amadori,
Che di rose e di fiori
Vi fate belle il maggio,

Venite alla frescura
Delli verdi arbuscelli.
Ogni bella è sicura
Fra tanti damigelli;
Chè le fiere e gli uccelli
Ardon d'amore il maggio.

Chi è giovane e bella
Deh non sie punto acerba,
Chè non si rinnovella
L'età, come fa l'erba:
Nessuna stia superba
All'amadore il maggio.

and beauty while youth lasts—follows Horace's *carpe diem* motif, which also prompted Lorenzo de Medici's "Triumph of Bacchus and Ariadne." But Poliziano displays a lightness of touch, an elegance of rhythm, a subtlety and a restraint which neither Lorenzo nor any other Italian poet of this period was ever quite able to achieve. With François Villon, Poliziano ranks as one of the two greatest European lyric poets of the fifteenth century.

"Welcome to May"

Welcome to May
And its wild banner :[1]

Welcome to spring
Which wants one to fall in love.
And you, young girls, in a group
With your sweethearts,
You who with roses and flowers
Make yourselves pretty in May,

Come to the cool shade
Of the green young trees.
Every pretty maiden is safe
Among so many youths;
For beasts and birds
Burn with love in May.

She who is young and beautiful,
Pray that she not be bitter,
For it does not renew itself,
Age—as does the grass:
Let no one remain proud
With her sweetheart in May.

[1] The "wild banner" was a branch which a young man would cut from a tree in the woods to attach to the door of his sweetheart's home on May Day.

Ciascuna balli e canti
Di questa schiera nostra.
Ecco che i dolci amanti
Van per voi, belle, in giostra:
Qual dura a lor si mostra
Farà sfiorire il maggio.

Per prender le donzelle
Si son gli amanti armati.
Arrendetevi, belle,
A' vostri innamorati;
Rendete i cuor furati,
Non fate guerra il maggio.

Chi l'altrui core invola
Ad altrui doni el core.
Ma chi è quel che vola?
È l'angiolel d'Amore,
Che viene a fare onore
Con voi, donzelle, al maggio.

Amor ne vien ridendo
Con rose e gigli in testa,
E vien di voi caendo.
Fategli, o belle, festa.
Qual sarà la più presta
A dargli e' fior del maggio?

Ben venga il peregrino.
Amor, che ne comandi?
Che al suo amante il crino
Ogni bella ingrillandi;
Chè le zitelle e grandi
S'innamoran di maggio.

Let each girl dance and sing
In this group of ours.
Behold your sweet lovers
Going, my pretty ones, to joust for you:
She who shows herself harsh to them
Will cause the withering of May.

To capture the young girls
Their lovers have armed themselves.
Surrender, my pretty ones,
To those in love with you;
Give back the hearts you have thieved,
Do not wage war in May.

Let her who has stolen someone's heart
Give her own heart in return.
But who is that one flying?
It's the young angel of Love,
Who is coming to do honor
With you, young girls, to May.

Love comes forth laughing
With roses and lilies on his head,
And he comes looking for you.
Greet him with joy, my pretty ones.
Which of you will be the first
To give him the flower of May?

Welcome to the pilgrim.
Love, what is your command?
That for her lover's hair
Each pretty one weave a garland;
For young girls and grown women
Fall in love in May.

Enea Vico
da Parma

Medaglia del
Don.

obiit A·C· 1533. Ætatis 69.

LUDOVICO ARIOSTO

(1474–1533)

DURING the first quarter of the sixteenth century, when Machiavelli, in Florence, was devoting himself to the analysis of ancient history and of contemporary political behavior, Ludovico Ariosto, in Ferrara, was composing the enchanting, musical octaves of his *Orlando Furioso*. This was an epic poem in 46 cantos, totaling about 40,000 lines, reminiscent of the *Chanson de Roland* and Arthurian romances as well as of such classics as the *Iliad*, the *Aeneid*, Ovid's *Metamorphoses*, and Seneca's *Hercules Furens*. It featured fantastic, breathtaking adventures, witches, monsters, magic castles, winged horses—a world which seemed completely removed from reality and reason. Machiavelli thought it possible to teach Italians concrete values, foremost among these the necessity of political unity which he so passionately advocated in the last chapter of *The Prince*. Ariosto, on the other hand, although living in one of the stormiest periods of Italian history, was as much disenchanted and unconcerned with national affairs as he was skeptical and indifferent in matters of morality and religion. As a poet, he was dedicated to the two supreme ideals of the Renaissance: art and beauty. *Orlando Furioso* was written, he stated, "for the amusement and recreation of gentlemen, persons with sensitive souls, and ladies."

Ariosto's absent-mindedness was proverbial (he allegedly went on a trip to Modena one day wearing his house slippers), yet he was also surprisingly practical and resourceful. His father, Count Niccolò Ariosto, administrator of the city of Ferrara for the Este family, died in 1500, leaving Ludovico, the eldest of ten children, in charge of the large household. To provide for the education and dowry of his brothers and sisters, the poet was compelled to join the staff of the House of Este. He spent most of his life in the service of the vicious, arrogant Cardinal Ippolito and of Duke Alfonso, who at one time sent him on a three-year tour of duty as governor of Garfagnana, a primitive, bandit-infested district of the Apennines. Ariosto hated being distracted from his studies and separated from Alessandra Benucci, his mistress. But he always managed to carry out with exceptional efficiency the various secretarial, diplomatic, and administrative functions he had to perform. Endowed with a naturally gentle and tolerant character, he resigned himself philosophically to the difficulties of his situation, which he depicted with humor and delicate irony in his *Satires*.

These same qualities of humor and irony, together with an extraordinary narrative power, make the *Orlando Furioso* a fascinating reading experience. The world of imagination and of sheer impossibility through which the story unfolds is always balanced by the poet's sense of reality and by the subtlety with which he implies that much that seems fictional and fantastic may well be possible after all.

Ariosto did not confine his hero, Orlando, to the traditional role of inflexible paladin and defender of the Faith. Far from it: in the *Furioso* Orlando forgets duty and honor and deserts the Christian army for love of Angelica, a beautiful pagan sorceress who had been sent to sow discord and havoc in the Christian camp. Blinded by passion, the noble knight pursues his beloved, but never manages to get hold of her, for besides being protected by magic, she hates men. One day, however, she too falls in love— with a young Saracen soldier, Medoro, whom she finds half dead on a battlefield and nurses back to life. Soon afterwards they are married in a shepherd's hut. Orlando, in his wandering, chances upon the hut and, unable to contain his despair at learning of the marriage, is driven into furious madness. Naked, brandishing a pole, he goes raving through France and Spain, destroying forests, slaughtering animals and men. Having crossed into Africa, he is finally subdued by a group of Christian knights, among whom is Astolfo, who has just returned from the moon with Orlando's brain in a bottle. Orlando is forced to inhale it and in that manner recovers his wits.

The *Orlando Furioso* quickly gained fame, not only in Italy, but also in France, Spain, and England. It is interesting to note that the eighteenth-century British statesman, Charles James Fox, urged his countrymen to learn Italian so that they could read this master-piece. Indeed, no translation can do justice to the particular linguistic texture of the *Furioso*, or to its glorious images and sounds.

The selection which follows describes the climactic moment in the poem when Orlando is overcome by madness.

La pazzia d'Orlando

(Orlando Furioso, *dal Canto XXIII°*)

Pel bosco errò tutta la notte il Conte;
E allo spuntar della diurna fiamma
Lo tornò il suo destin sopra la fonte
Dove Medoro insculse l'epigramma.
Veder l'ingiuria sua scritta nel monte
L'accese sì, ch'in lui non restò dramma
Che non fosse odio, rabbia, ira e furore;
Nè più indugiò, che trasse il brando fuore.

Tagliò lo scritto e il sasso, e sino al cielo
A volo alzar fe' le minute schegge.
Infelice quell'antro, ed ogni stelo
In cui Medoro e Angelica si legge!
Così restâr quel dì, ch'ombra nè gelo
A pastor mai non daran più, nè a gregge:
E quella fonte, già sì chiara e pura,
Da cotanta ira fu poco sicura;

Che rami e ceppi e tronchi e sassi e zolle
Non cessò di gittar ne le bell'onde,
Fin che da sommo ad imo sì turbolle,
Che non furo mai più chiare nè monde;
E stanco alfin, e al fin di sudor molle,
Poi che la lena vinta non risponde
Allo sdegno, al grande odio, all'ardente ira,
Cade sul prato, e verso il ciel sospira.

Orlando's Madness

(*Orlando Furioso*, from Canto XXIII)

The count wandered all night through the woods;
And at the rising of the flame of day
His destiny took him back to the spring
Where Medoro had carved his inscription.[1]
The sight of this insult written on the mountain
Inflamed him so, that not one dram remained in him
Which was not hatred, rage, wrath, and fury;
Nor did he delay, but drew his sword.

He slashed the writing and the rock, and up to the sky
Made their minute splinters rise in flight.
Unhappy that cave and every bole
Where "Medoro and Angelica" was to be read!
They were left that day in such a state, that neither shade
    nor coolness
Will they ever again provide to shepherd or flock:
And that spring, once so clear and pure,
Was not at all safe from such great wrath;

For branches and logs and tree trunks and stones and clods
He kept throwing into those lovely waves,
Until he had troubled them from top to bottom in such a way
That they were never again clear or clean;
And tired at last, and at last made limp by sweat,
Since his vanquished strength responds no more
To his disdain, his great hatred, his burning wrath,
He falls in the meadow, and sighs toward the sky.

[1] After his marriage to Angelica in a shepherd's hut, Medoro had carved their names on the surrounding trees and mountains.

Afflitto e stanco al fin cade ne l'erba,
E ficca gli occhi al cielo, e non fa motto.
Senza cibo e dormir così si serba,
Che 'l sole esce tre volte, e torna sotto.
Di crescer non cessò la pena acerba,
Che fuor del senno al fin l'ebbe condotto.
Il quarto dì da gran furor commosso
E maglie e piastre si stracciò di dosso.

Qui riman l'elmo, e là riman lo scudo,
Lontan gli arnesi, e più lontan l'usbergo:
L'arme sue tutte, in somma vi concludo,
Avean pel bosco differente albergo.
E poi si squarciò i panni, e mostrò ignudo
L'ispido ventre, e tutto 'l petto e 'l tergo;
E cominciò la gran follia, sì orrenda,
Che de la più non sarà mai ch'intenda.

In tanta rabbia, in tanto furor venne,
Che rimase offuscato in ogni senso.
Di tôr la spada in man non gli sovvenne;
Che fatte avria mirabil cose, penso.
Ma nè quella nè scure nè bipenne
Era bisogno al suo vigore immenso.
Quivi fe' ben de le sue prove eccelse;
Ch'un alto pino al primo crollo svelse:

E svelse dopo il primo altri parecchi,
Come fosser finocchi, ebuli o aneti;
E fe' il simil di querce e d'olmi vecchi,
Di faggi e d'orni e d'ilici e d'abeti.
Quel, ch'un uccellator che s'apparecchi
Il campo mondo, fa, per por le reti,
Dei giunchi e de le stoppie e de l'urtiche,
Facea de' cerri e d'altre piante antiche.

Wretched and tired at last, he falls in the grass,
And stares fixedly at the sky, and does not utter a word.
So he remains without food or sleep,
While the sun comes up three times, and goes back down.
His harsh pain did not cease growing
Until at last it led him out of his mind.
On the fourth day, stirred by great fury,
He tore off his coat of mail and his breastplates.

Here lies his helmet, and there lies his shield,
Far away his battle gear, and farther still his *hauberk*:
All his armor, in short, I conclude,
Had different residences in the woods.
And then he ripped open his clothes, and bared
His shaggy belly, and all his chest and back;
And the great madness began, so horrendous,
That no man will ever hear of a greater one.

He went into such rage, into such fury,
That all his senses were befogged.
He did not remember to take his sword in hand;
For he would have done marvelous things, I think.
But neither sword nor hatchet nor double axe
Did his immense vigor require.
Right there he gave mighty proofs of it;
For he uprooted a tall pine at the first pull:

And after the first he uprooted several others,
As though they were fennel, danewort, or dill;
And he did the same with aged oaks and elms,
With beech and ash and ilex and fir trees.
What a bird hunter, when he sets out
To clear his field to lay his nets,
Does with reeds and stubble and nettles,
[Orlando] did with great oaks and other ancient trees.

MICHELANGELO BUONARROTI

(1475–1564)

MOST of Michelangelo's two hundred sonnets and madrigals were composed between his sixtieth and his eightieth year—a rare instance of a man's power to create outstanding lyric poetry late in life.

Born in the Tuscan town of Caprese, Michelangelo studied under the patronage of Lorenzo de' Medici. While living in Florence, he met Marsilio Ficino and soon was an advocate of neo-Platonic philosophy, which later became a major source of inspiration for his poetry. In 1534 he settled permanently in Rome, and it was there, when working on the Last Judgment and the huge frescoes in the Pauline Chapel, that he—then in his sixties—met the poetess Vittoria Colonna and a young nobleman, Tommaso Cavalieri. To them he dedicated some of his best love poems, Platonically exalting their beauty, which to him was living proof of the immanence of the divine on earth. The sonnet "Veggio nel tuo bel viso," in which Tommaso Cavalieri is called "Signore"—Lord—is perhaps the highest and most moving achievement of Michelangelo as a poet.

Michelangelo's verse is often difficult, at least on first reading; at times it seems too intellectual and hermetic. But it has a solemn grandeur, an incisiveness, and a ring of sincerity which place it clearly above the shallow Petrarchesque compositions of most sixteenth-century poets. Francesco Berni (see pp. 81–83) pointed out the difference between Michelangelo and his contemporaries in a famous line: "Ei dice cose, e voi dite parole"—"He says things and you say words."

Only occasionally, especially in the few poems composed when he was still young, did Michelangelo approach poetry in a light vein. When he did, he revealed a surprising talent for humorous, comic effects. The tailed sonnet "I' ho già fatto un gozzo,"

"Veggio nel tuo bel viso, Signor mio"

Veggio nel tuo bel viso, Signor mio,
Quel che narrar mal puossi in questa vita.
L'anima della carne ancor vestita,
Con esso è già più volte ascesa a Dio.
E se 'l vulgo malvagio, isciocco e rio
Di quel che sente altrui segna e addita,
Non è l'intensa voglia men gradita,
L'amor, la fede e l'onesto desio.

A quel pietoso fonte, onde siam tutti,
S'assembra ogni beltà che qua si vede,
Più c'altra cosa alle persone accorte;
Nè altro saggio abbiam, nè altri frutti
Del cielo in terra; e chi v'ama con fede
Trascende a Dio, e fa dolce la morte.

which he wrote in 1509 while painting the vault of the Sistine
Chapel, is a vivid, amusing self-portrait of the master perched on
his scaffold, straining to keep his balance, his body contorted,
his mind numbed by the pain of the physical effort.

"I see in your handsome face, my Lord"

I see in your handsome face, my Lord,
What one can ill describe in this life.
My soul, still clothed in flesh,
With that [face] has already ascended many times to God.
And though the malevolent, foolish, and wicked crowd
Notes and points a finger at what others feel,
Intense craving pleases no less,
Nor do love, faith, and honest desire.

That fount of mercy, whence we all exist,
Every beauty seen here [on earth] resembles,
More than anything else to knowing persons;
Nor do we have other evidence, or other fruit
Of heaven upon earth; and he who loves you with faith
Transcends to God, and makes death sweet.

A Giovanni da Pistoia quando l'autore dipingeva la volta della Sistina, 1509

I' ho già fatto un gozzo in questo stento,
Come fa l'acqua a' gatti in Lombardia,
O ver d'altro paese che si sia,
Ch'a forza 'l ventre appicca sotto 'l mento.
La barba al cielo, e la memoria sento
In sullo scrigno, e'l petto fo d'arpia:
E 'l pennel sopra 'l viso tuttavia
Mel fa, gocciando, un ricco pavimento.

E lombi entrati mi son nella peccia,
E fo del cul per contrappeso groppa,
E' passi senza gli occhi muovo invano.
Dinanzi mi s'allunga la corteccia,
E per piegarsi addietro si ragroppa,
E tendomi com'arco soriano.

Però fallace e strano
Surge il iudizio che la mente porta;
Chè mal si tra' per cerbottana torta.

La mia pittura morta
Difendi orma', Giovanni, e'l mio onore,
Non sendo in loco bon, nè io pittore.

To Giovanni da Pistoia When the Author Was Painting the Vault of the Sistine Chapel, 1509

I have already grown a goitre in this drudgery—
As water does to cats in Lombardy,
Or in whatever other region it may be—
Which forces my belly to hang under my chin.
I feel my beard skyward, and memory
On top of my coffer,[1] and my chest like a harpy's;
And on my face all the while the brush
With its dripping makes a rich pavement.

My loins have entered my paunch,
And I turn my arse into a croup for a counterweight,
And I take steps vainly without my eyes.
My bark[2] stretches out in front,
And from wrinkling in back, is all knotted,
And I strain like a Syrian bow.

Thus fallacious and strange
Rises the judgment which my mind carries;
For one shoots badly through a crooked blowpipe.

My dead painting
Defend now, Giovanni, and my honor,
For I am not in a good place, nor am I a painter.

[1] A slang figure for "back."
[2] A slang figure for "skin."

FRANCESCO BERNI

(1497–1535)

THE influence of Petrarch's poetry on Italian literature was never more widespread than during the sixteenth century. Editions of his *Canzoniere* appeared in great number, and scores of poets thought it fashionable to write in Petrarchan style of their ladies' beautiful eyes, lovely hands, golden hair, and of lovers' melancholic solitude. The most famous of these poets was Pietro Bembo, revered by admiring contemporaries as "the Venetian Petrarch." Bembo's lyrics were mostly sonnets, perfectly wrought, but quite evidently the result of skillful mannerism.

Francesco Berni, a Tuscan from Lamporecchio, reacted against Petrarchan imitators, ridiculing them and parodying their compositions. He showed a predilection for trivial themes— the praise of peaches, of eels, of jelly, of a warm bed, of the popular card game *primiera*. In a famous terza rima poem he described in detail the discomforts of a night spent in the filthy home of a priest; in another, dedicated to Aristotle, he noted that the philosopher's works were regrettably incomplete since they did not include a cookbook.

Berni's sharp wit and gift for caricature gave birth to a new genre of burlesque and satiric poetry, still called "Bernesque." His best-known poem, our selection "Chiome d'argento fine, irte ed attorte," is not only an impressive catalogue of feminine ugliness and a deliberate parody of a sonnet in which Bembo, imitating Petrarch, extolled the charms of his lady; it is also an example of great subtlety in the choice and counterpointing of words.

Berni's signal gift for poking fun at his contemporaries—including those in high places, such as Popes Hadrian VI and Clement VII—inevitably brought him powerful enemies. His life ended tragically; he was poisoned in his thirty-eighth year,

"Chiome d'argento fine, irte ed attorte"

Chiome d'argento fine, irte ed attorte
Senz'arte intorno ad un bel viso d'oro:
Fronte crespa, u' mirando io mi scoloro,
Dove spuntan gli strali Amore e Morte.
Occhi di perle vaghi, luci torte
Da ogni obbietto diseguale a loro:
Ciglia di neve, e quelle, ond'io m'accoro,
Dita e man dolcemente grosse e corte.

Labbra di latte, bocca ampia celeste,
Denti d'ebano rari e pellegrini,
Inaudita ineffabile armonia;
Costumi alteri e gravi; a voi, divini
Servi d'Amor, palese fo che queste
Son le bellezze della donna mia.

apparently by either Cardinal Ippolito de' Medici or Duke Alessandro, both of whom had tried in vain to enlist the poet's support in their bitter struggle for power in Florence.

"Hair of fine silver, shaggy and twisted"

Hair of fine silver, shaggy and twisted
Tastelessly around a beautiful face of gold:
Wrinkled brow, gazing at which I pale,
Whereon Love and Death break their arrow points.
Shimmering eyes of pearl, beams turned away
By every object unequal to them;
Eyebrows of snow, and you, which move my heart,
Fingers and hands, delightfully thick and short.

Lips of milk, large azure mouth,
Teeth of ebony, rare and wandering,
Unheard of, ineffable harmony;
Manners haughty and ponderous; to you, divine
Servants of Love, I now make plain that such
Are the charms of my lady.

TORQUATO TASSO

(1544–1595)

ALTHOUGH Torquato Tasso is better known as a writer of epics because of his *Gerusalemme Liberata*, a heroic poem set against the background of the first Crusade, his highest achievements are nevertheless to be found in lyric compositions: many passages of the *Gerusalemme* itself, the beautiful pastoral play *Aminta* (Amyntas), and the love poems in his collected *Rime*.

At the age of twenty-one Tasso entered the service of the Este family of Ferrara, just as Ariosto had done before him at the turn of the century. But unlike Ariosto's, Tasso's association with the House of Este was a tragic one. In 1575, after having completed his major works, Tasso suffered the first of a series of nervous breakdowns that very rapidly took the form of furious insanity and required first isolation in the Este palace and a monastery, and later confinement in the asylum of Sant'Anna, where on occasion he had to be kept in chains. The popular legend, the basis of Goethe's drama *Torquato Tasso*, whereby the poet's confinement at Sant'Anna was the consequence of a love affair with the Duke of Este's sister Leonora, has been proved unfounded. The real cause of Tasso's mental illness seems to have been a deep-rooted feeling of insecurity. He was obsessed by religious doubts (time and again he sought to be examined by the Inquisition as a heretic) and by feelings of persecution that made him uncontrollably fearful of any adverse criticism of his work. Tasso remained at Sant'Anna seven years. Released in 1586, but not fully cured, he spent the rest of his life wandering from city to city, never at peace with himself. He died in Rome, in the monastery of Saint Onofrio.

Our four selections, three madrigals and one lament, are typical examples of Tasso's lyric vein at its best. The first two, like many other of his love poems, were written for a young girl of noble extraction, Laura Peperara, whom Tasso met in Mantua in 1564. The play between the name of Laura and the word "l'aura"—"the breeze" (in the singular form in the first poem, lines 3 and 13; in the plural in the second, line 10)—is reminiscent of Petrarch. However, what is striking about these poems

"Ecco mormorar l'onde"

Ecco mormorar l'onde,
E tremolar le fronde
A l'aura mattutina, e gli arboscelli,
E sovra i verdi rami i vaghi augelli
Cantar soavemente,
E rider l'Oriente;
Ecco già l'alba appare,
E si specchia nel mare,
E rasserena il cielo,
E le campagne imperla il dolce gelo,
E gli alti monti indora:
O bella e vaga Aurora,
L'aura è tua messaggera, e tu de l'aura
Ch'ogni arso cor ristaura.

is not the imitation of Petrarchan themes or devices but rather Tasso's interest in musical effects. His main concern was clearly not with thoughts or ideas but with images and words, which he chose with great care and precision primarily for their capacity to captivate the attention with the magic of their sounds. In this respect Tasso is the precursor of "pure" poetry, and many a poet of the nineteenth and twentieth centuries, from Leopardi to Ungaretti, is considerably indebted to him.

"Now the waves murmur"

Now the waves murmur
And the boughs and the shrubs tremble
in the morning breeze,
And on the green branches the pleasant birds
Sing softly
And the east smiles;
Now dawn already appears
And mirrors herself in the sea,
And makes the sky serene,
And the gentle frost impearls the fields
And gilds the high mountains:
O beautiful and gracious Aurora,
The breeze is your messenger, and you the breeze's
Which revives each burnt-out heart.

"Qual rugiada o qual pianto"

Qual rugiada o qual pianto,
Quai lagrime eran quelle
Che sparger vidi dal notturno manto
E dal candido volto delle stelle?
E perchè seminò la bianca luna
Di cristalline stelle un puro nembo
A l'erba fresca in grembo?
Perchè nell'aria bruna
S'udian, quasi dolendo, intorno intorno
Gir l'aure insino al giorno?
Fur segni forse della tua partita,
Vita della mia vita?

"Tacciono i boschi e i fiumi"

Tacciono i boschi e i fiumi,
E 'l mar senza onda giace,
Ne le spelonche i venti han tregua e pace,
E ne la notte bruna
Alto silenzio fa la bianca luna;
E noi tegnamo ascose
Le dolcezze amorose:
Amor non parli o spiri,
Sien muti i baci e muti i miei sospiri.

"What dew or what weeping"

What dew or what weeping,
What tears were those
I saw scattered from night's mantle
And from the pale face of the stars?
And why did the white moon sow
A pure cloud of crystalline stars
In the lap of the fresh grass?
Why in the dark air
Could one hear, almost lamenting, around and
*   around*
The breezes roaming till daybreak?
Were they perhaps signs of your departure,
Life of my life?

"The woods and the rivers are silent"

The woods and the rivers are silent,
And the waveless sea is at rest;
In their caves the winds are at truce and peace,
And in the dark night
The white moon creates lofty silence;
And we keep hidden
The sweetnesses of love:
Let love not speak or breathe,
Let kisses be soundless, and soundless my sighs.

"Un'ape esser vorrei"

Un'ape esser vorrei,
Donna bella e crudele,
Che susurrando in voi suggesse il mèle
E, non potendo il cor, potesse almeno
Pungervi 'l bianco seno
E 'n sì dolce ferita
Vendicata lasciar la propria vita.

"I'd like to be a bee"

I'd like to be a bee,
O beautiful cruel lady,
Who, murmuring, would suck the honey in
     you,
And, being unable [to sting] your heart,
     could at least
Sting your white breast
And in so sweet a wound
Leave its own life, avenged.

IL. CAVALIER MARINO D'ETA D'ANNI LVI.

Si tua vita, Marine, leues est lapsa per vmbras,
Clarior ex vmbris en tibi vita redit.

GIAMBATTISTA MARINO

(1569–1625)

THE seventeenth century is regarded in Italian literature as a period of decadence whose main traits are frequently epitomized in one word: "Marinism." The term, derived from the name of Giambattista Marino, implies a special attitude toward literature in general and poetry in particular. The poet's aim is no longer to teach, to enlighten, or simply to please the reader; it is, in Marino's own formulation, to produce surprise, the marvelous: "È del poeta il fin la meraviglia." And how will a poet create the marvelous? By using all manner of far-fetched images, telescoped metaphors, hyperbolic sentences, synonyms, antonyms, alliterations.

All such devices abound in Marino's poetry. For instance, in his chief work, *Adone*, a mythological poem over forty thousand lines long about the love of Venus for Adonis, we find dawn described as a "beautiful nurse" rising "from purple feathers to feed with her heavenly humors grass, plants, and flowers." And in his famous "Canzone dei baci" (The Song of Kisses), the words "bacio" (kiss), "baciare" (to kiss), and "bocca" (mouth), are monotonously intermeshed again and again in all possible combinations and patterns.

But not everything that Marino wrote is extravagant conceit, tiresome tirade, empty sound effect. Especially among his numerous love poems (Marino had many love affairs: in one lyric he confessed that all women made him "burn with desire") there are quite a few compositions that reveal an uncommon gift for creating fresh images and for portraying original situations.

Our selection, "Bella schiava," describing the poet's passion for a black servant, is a case in point.

Marino was celebrated as the greatest Italian poet of his time. He lived in Naples, his native city, until 1600. In that year, after being imprisoned a second time for disorderly conduct, he escaped and went to Rome. From Rome he moved to Turin, to the court of Carl Emmanuel of Savoy, and from there to Paris in 1615. It was in France that Marino's fame reached its apogee. He

Bella schiava

Nera sì, ma se' bella, o di Natura
Fra le belle d'Amor leggiadro mostro.
Fosca è l'alba appo te; perde e s'oscura
Presso l'ebeno tuo l'avorio e l'ostro.
Or quando, or dove il mondo antico o il nostro
Vide sì viva mai, sentì sì pura
O luce uscir di tenebroso inchiostro,
O di spento carbon nascere arsura?

Servo di chi m'è serva, ecco ch'avvolto
Porto di bruno laccio il core intorno,
Che per candida man non fia mai sciolto.
Là 've più ardi, o Sol, sol per tuo scorno
Un sole è nato; un Sol, che nel bel volto
Porta la notte ed ha negli occhi il giorno.

lived at the court of the Queen, Maria de' Medici, and to her, in 1623, he dedicated his poem *Adone*, which was acclaimed as an unsurpassable masterpiece. Soon afterward Marino returned to Italy, greeted with triumphant receptions in every city he visited. Covered with glory, he spent the remaining two years of his life in Naples. The impact of his influence can be detected not only in the works of several minor Italian writers, but also in the writings of poets such as Crashaw in Great Britain and Góngora in Spain.

Beautiful Slave

Black—yes, but you are beautiful, O Nature's
Graceful exhibit among Love's beauties.
Dawn is gloomy alongside you; defeated and darkened
Are ivory and crimson by your ebony.
When or where did the ancient world, or ours,
Ever see such lively, ever feel such pure
Light coming out of dark ink,
Or such ardor issuing from spent coal?

Servant of her who is my servant, here I am
bearing my heart caught in a brown noose
Which can never be untied by a pure-white hand.
There where you burn the most, O Sun, for your shame alone
A sun has been born; a Sun who in her beautiful face
Bears the night, and in her eyes has day.

UGO FOSCOLO

(1778–1827)

THE general decline in the field of Italian lyric poetry during the seventeenth century extended well into the next. Indeed, it is not until the end of the eighteenth century that one encounters the figure of a major poet: Ugo Foscolo.

Foscolo was born on the Greek island of Zante, a Venetian possession in the Ionian Sea. His father was a doctor of Venetian extraction; his mother was Greek. In 1793, after his father's death, Foscolo went to Venice. This was the first of a long sequence of peregrinations characterizing his turbulent life. An ardent admirer of the French Revolution, he wrote an ode in 1796 hailing Napoleon as the "Liberator of Italy." However, a year later, when Napoleon ceded Venice and its territory to Austria, Foscolo turned bitterly against him and fled to Milan. The disillusionment suffered on that occasion emerges as one of the two dominant themes (the other being a tragic love affair) of *Le ultime lettere di Jacopo Ortis* (The Last Letters of Jacopo Ortis), a largely autobiographical novel published in Milan in 1802. Foscolo lived mostly in Milan until 1804, then for two years in France as a captain in the Italian Division attached to the French Army. During that time he translated Sterne's *Sentimental Journey* in an Italian version that ranks as one of the most brilliant prose translations in a Western language. Back in Italy, in 1807 he published his best-known work, "Dei sepolcri" (On Tombs), a long poem in blank verse passionately advocating the preservation of the tombs of great men of the past as a source of inspiration and guidance for the living. Subsequent to the appearance of "Dei sepolcri" Foscolo's fame grew incessantly, and he was asked to take the chair of Italian Rhetoric at the University of Pavia. Then in 1815 the Austrian authorities who had reoccupied Milan after Napoleon's downfall offered Foscolo the editorship of a literary journal, on condition that he swear allegiance to Austria. Foscolo refused, choosing instead voluntary exile, first in Switzerland, later in London. He spent the last eleven years of his life in England, where he enjoyed a brief period of affluence and of considerable social and literary prominence. But his extravagance soon brought him to complete ruin. On one occasion he was even imprisoned for debt, and he died penniless and forgotten in a slum of Turnham Green on the Thames. Forty-four years after his death his remains were taken to Florence and buried in the Church of Santa Croce alongside Machiavelli, Michelangelo, and Galileo, whose tombs he had celebrated in his "Sepolcri."

Alla sera

Forse perchè della fatal quiete
Tu sei l'imago a me sì cara vieni,
O sera! E quando ti corteggian liete
Le nubi estive e i zeffiri sereni,
E quando dal nevoso aere inquiete
Tenebre e lunghe all'universo meni
Sempre scendi invocata, e le secrete
Vie del mio cor soavemente tieni.

Vagar mi fai co' miei pensier su l'orme
Che vanno al nulla eterno; e intanto fugge
Questo reo tempo, e van con lui le torme
Delle cure onde meco egli si strugge;
E mentre io guardo la tua pace, dorme
Quello spirto guerrier ch'entro mi rugge.

Foscolo's output in verse was by no means voluminous. In addition to the works already mentioned, he wrote "Le grazie" (The Graces), a three-part allegorical poem which he left unfinished, three tragedies, two odes, and twelve sonnets. These sonnets alone, however, are enough to assure him a place of distinction among Italian poets. "Alla sera" (To Evening) and "In morte del fratello Giovanni" (Upon the Death of His Brother Giovanni), here included, are two of the most perfect poems in Italian literature. Of obvious romantic inspiration, they were composed at approximately the same time as *Le ultime lettere di Jacopo Ortis*, and like this novel give vivid expression to the poet's restless nature, his longing for peace, and his meditations on death. "In morte del fratello Giovanni," reminiscent of a poem by Catullus, was written in 1801 when Foscolo, a fugitive in Milan, learned of his brother's suicide in Venice.

To Evening

Perhaps because you are the image
of the fatal quiet, your coming is so dear to me,
O evening! And whether gay summer clouds
and serene zephyrs court you,
Or whether down from the snowy air
you bring long, restless nights to the world,
Always you descend invoked,
and you softly take hold of the secret paths of my heart.

You cause me to wander with my thoughts upon the traces
That lead to eternal nothingness; and meanwhile
this evil time flees, and with it go the swarms
Of cares with which it is destroying itself and me;
And the while I gaze upon your peacefulness
that warrior spirit which roars in me is sleeping.

In morte del fratello Giovanni

Un dì, s'io non andrò sempre fuggendo
Di gente in gente, mi vedrai seduto
Su la tua pietra, o fratel mio, gemendo
Il fior dei tuoi gentili anni caduto.
La madre or sol, suo dì tardo traendo,
Parla di me col tuo cenere muto:
Ma io deluse a voi le palme tendo;
E se da lunge i miei tetti saluto,

Sento gli avversi Numi, e le secrete
Cure che al viver tuo furon tempesta,
E prego anch'io nel tuo porto quiete.
Questo di tanta speme oggi mi resta!
Straniere genti, l'ossa mie rendete
Allora al petto della madre mesta.

Upon the Death of His Brother Giovanni

One day, if I am not to keep on fleeing
From people to people, you will see me seated
On your stone, O my brother, weeping
For the fallen flower of your gentle years.
Our mother, alone now, drawing out her late day,
Speaks about me to your mute ashes:
But [as for me] I stretch out deluded palms toward you
And even though I greet my [home's] roofs from afar,

I feel the hostile Gods, and the secret
Cares that were a tempest to your life,
And I too pray for the quietness of your haven.
This is all that remains to me today of so much hope!
Foreign peoples, when the time comes, give back my bones
to the bosom of my grieving mother!

GIACOMO LEOPARDI

(1798–1837)

GIACOMO LEOPARDI, one of the greatest Italian poets of all times, was born in Recanati, a town in the Marches not far from the Adriatic coast. The Leopardis were of the nobility; Giacomo's father was a count, his mother a marchioness— both rigid, narrow-minded aristocrats. The mother in particular, absorbed by the administration of the dwindling family patrimony, never quite managed to understand her sensitive, precocious son or to give him the affection he needed.

At the age of twelve Giacomo was so erudite that his private ecclesiastical tutor had to admit that his own scholarship was inferior to his pupil's and that consequently there was nothing more he could teach him. Devoured by an insatiable craving for learning, Giacomo then resolved to continue his studies alone, and for the next seven years, completely unsupervised, spent most of the day and part of the night poring over the books of the family palace's twelve-thousand-volume library. He mastered Hebrew, Latin, Greek, and modern languages; completed numerous translations from the classics; wrote several philological works, a history of astronomy, and a hymn to Neptune in Greek which he pretended to have discovered in an ancient manuscript. By the time he was nineteen years old he had amassed an amazing store of knowledge, but he had also compromised his health: he began suffering from nervous disorders, his eyesight weakened, he became a hunchback. Sadly he realized that he had allowed his youth to pass, that henceforth his life could be only unhappy, and that, above all, being so frail and unattractive, he would probably never be loved by a woman. He felt it would require great courage "to love a virtuous man whose only beauty is the soul." These pessimistic thoughts and premonitions which he poured out in a letter to the critic Pietro Giordani on March 2, 1818, pervade all of Leopardi's major works: from the *Canti* (Songs), his masterpiece, composed at various intervals during his life, to the *Operette morali* (Little Moral Works), a collection of prose writings in dialogue and essay form, and from the monumental *Zibaldone* (Miscellaneous Thoughts), perhaps the most fascinating diary ever kept, to the rich *Epistolario* (Letters), both published posthumously.

A typical example of Leopardi's pessimistic conception of life is "La quiete dopo la tempesta" (The Calm after the Storm), here included. After a masterful description of a lively country scene, recorded in an impressionistic manner and full of movement and rhythm, the poet almost cruelly stresses his belief that joy is nothing but the momentary subsidence of pain and that

L'infinito

Sempre caro mi fu quest'ermo colle,
E questa siepe, che da tanta parte
Dell'ultimo orizzonte il guardo esclude.
Ma sedendo e mirando, interminati
Spazi di là da quella, e sovrumani
Silenzi, e profondissima quiete
Io nel pensier mi fingo; ove per poco
Il cor non si spaura. E come il vento
Odo stormir tra queste piante, io quello
Infinito silenzio a questa voce
Vo comparando: e mi sovvien l'eterno,
E le morte stagioni, e la presente
E viva, e il suon di lei. Così tra questa
Immensità s'annega il pensier mio:
E il naufragar m'è dolce in questo mare.

only in death can man find lasting happiness. But although statements in this vein appear frequently in the *Canti*, they are balanced by many others—such as the wonderful last line of "L'infinito" (The Infinite): "E il naufragar m'è dolce in questo mare" (And to shipwreck is sweet for me in this sea)—that uncover a completely different aspect of Leopardi: not the optimist, to be sure, but the enraptured admirer of nature's beauty, and the believer in the power of the imagination.

"L'infinito," our first selection, represents one of the summits not only of Leopardi's poetry but of all poetry. Rarely has a poet been able to compress within one hundred words such depth of meaning with such simplicity of language and harmony of sounds. Leopardi called "L'infinito" an "idyll," a definition that perfectly fits the charm and suggestive power of this superb poem, which, to quote Renato Poggioli, "makes familiar and almost dear to the heart of man the alien metaphysical vision of a universe ruled by laws other than those of life and death."

The Infinite

Always dear to me was this lonely hill,
And this hedge, which from so great a part
Of the farthest horizon excludes the gaze.
But as I sit and watch, I invent in my mind
endless spaces beyond, and superhuman
silences, and profoundest quiet;
wherefore my heart
almost loses itself in fear. And as I hear the wind
rustle through these plants, I compare
that infinite silence to this voice:
and I recall to mind eternity,
And the dead seasons, and the one present
And alive, and the sound of it. So in this
Immensity my thinking drowns:
And to shipwreck is sweet for me in this sea.

La quiete dopo la tempesta

Passata è la tempesta:
Odo augelli far festa, e la gallina,
Tornata in su la via,
Che ripete il suo verso. Ecco il sereno
Rompe là da ponente, alla montagna;
Sgombrasi la campagna,
E chiaro nella valle il fiume appare.
Ogni cor si rallegra, in ogni lato
Risorge il romorio,
Torna il lavoro usato.
L'artigiano a mirar l'umido cielo,
Con l'opra in man, cantando,
Fassi in su l'uscio; a prova
Vien fuor la femminetta a côr dell'acqua
Della novella piova;
E l'erbaiuol rinnova
Di sentiero in sentiero
Il grido giornaliero.
Ecco il Sol che ritorna, ecco sorride
Per li poggi e le ville. Apre i balconi,
Apre terrazzi e logge la famiglia:
E, dalla via corrente, odi lontano
Tintinnio di sonagli; il carro stride
Del passegger che il suo cammin ripiglia.
Si rallegra ogni core.
Sì dolce, sì gradita
Quand'è, com'or, la vita?
Quando con tanto amore
L'uomo a' suoi studi intende?
O torna all'opre? o cosa nova imprende?
Quando de' mali suoi men si ricorda?
Piacer figlio d'affanno;
Gioia vana, ch'è frutto
Del passato timore, onde si scosse
E paventò la morte

The Calm after the Storm

The storm has passed:
I hear birds rejoicing, and the hen,
Back again in the road,
Repeating her refrain. Look! the blue sky
Breaks through, there, from the west toward the
    mountain;
The countryside sweeps free,
And the bright river comes into view in the valley.
Every heart gladdens, everywhere
A busy sound resurges,
Customary tasks resume.
The craftsman, to gaze at the humid sky,
With his work in his hand, singing,
Comes to the door. Vying [with her companions],
A girl comes out to gather water
From the new rainfall;
And the vegetable vendor renews
From footpath to footpath
His daily cry.
Look! the sun returns. Look! it smiles
On the hills and villages. Servants open the balconies,
open terraces and loggias;
And you hear far away, from the main road,
A tinkling of bells; the traveler's cart
screeches as he takes up his journey again.
Every heart gladdens.
When else is life
so sweet, so pleasing as now?
When else with so much love
Does man turn to his pursuits?
Or resume his tasks? Or undertake something new?
When does he remember his misfortunes less?
Pleasure: child of anxiety:
An empty joy, the fruit
Of past fear whence
one who abhorred life

Chi la vita abborria;
Onde in lungo tormento,
Fredde, tacite, smorte,
Sudar le genti e palpitar, vedendo
Mossi alle nostre offese
Folgori, nembi e vento.

O natura cortese,
Son questi i doni tuoi,
Questi i diletti sono
Che tu porgi ai mortali. Uscir di pena
È diletto fra noi.
Pene tu spargi a larga mano; il duolo
Spontaneo sorge: e di piacer, quel tanto
Che per mostro e miracolo talvolta
Nasce d'affanno, è gran guadagno. Umana
Prole cara agli eterni! assai felice
Se respirar ti lice
D'alcun dolor: beata
Se te d'ogni dolor morte risana.

was startled into fearing death;
Whence in long travail,
Cold, silent, pale,
People sweated and trembled as they saw
lightning, clouds, and winds
moving to attack us.

O generous Nature,
These are your gifts,
These are the delights
That you offer to us mortals. To be relieved from pain
Is delight for us.
You spread pains with a free hand; grief
Springs up spontaneously; and that token of pleasure
Which by prodigy and miracle at times
Is born of anxiety, is a great gain. O human
Progeny dear to the eternal ones! Happy indeed
If you are allowed to recover your breath
After some grief; blessed
If death heals every grief.

GABRIELE D'ANNUNZIO

(1863-1938)

IT would be difficult to single out an Italian literary figure
whose exuberance, flamboyance, and fascination as a man and
whose prolific output as an author surpass Gabriele D'Annunzio's.
He was a poet, novelist, playwright, and journalist who enjoyed
resounding success in his own lifetime; a member of Parliament
at thirty-four; a daring flyer, naval commander and infantry
leader who, while in his fifties, performed astounding feats in
war; a commoner who at sixty-one had the title of Prince be-
stowed upon him by King Victor Emmanuel III; and throughout
his multifarious career a dashing and tireless conqueror of ladies'
hearts.

D'Annunzio was born in the Adriatic city of Pescara. By the
time he was nineteen he had published two books of verse—
Primo vere (In Early Spring) and *Canto novo* (New Song)—and
one volume of short stories, *Terra vergine* (Virgin Land). An un-
titled Alcaic ode from *Canto novo* provides a vivid insight into
the elemental philosophical and aesthetic creed that guided his
life. The two opening stanzas, literally translated, read thus:

> Sing of joy! I want to wreathe you
> With every flower so that you may celebrate
> Joy, Joy, Joy,
> This magnificent giver!
>
> Sing of the immense joy of living,
> Of being strong, of being young,
> Of biting the fruits of the earth
> With firm, white, voracious teeth . . .

D'Annunzio was fundamentally a hedonist, pursuing the pleasures of life in all the forms available to him. This quest for pleasure manifests itself in his poetry not only in the most familiar themes (the pantheistic exaltation of nature, of instinct, and of physical love, and the celebration of the Nietzschean ideal of the superman) but also in his predilection for opulent words, dazzling titles and phrases, sensuous onomatopoeias and rhythms.

D'Annunzio was endowed with seemingly inexhaustible energy and an unlimited capacity for creative writing. The national edition of his works, undertaken at government expense, totals forty-nine volumes. As we approach his vast production today, however, we find that a very substantial portion of it has not weathered too well the passage of time. This is not to say that there is not in his work, and especially in his poetry, much that is fine and lasting. A modern critic has suggested that D'Annunzio's poetry be rescued from the mausoleum of his complete works. To be sure, pieces of excellent poetry emerge from the thousands

La pioggia nel pineto

Taci. Su le soglie
Del bosco non odo
Parole che dici
Umane; ma odo
Parole piu nuove
Che parlano gocciole e foglie
Lontane.
Ascolta. Piove
Dalle nuvole sparse.
Piove su le tamerici
Salmastre ed arse,
Piove su i pini
Scagliosi ed irti,
Piove su i mirti
Divini,

and thousands of pages. One such piece is our selection "La pioggia nel pineto" (Rain in the Pine Wood), a poem of love and identification with nature, a striking symphony of sound-words vaguely reminiscent of Debussy's music. "La pioggia nel pineto" is taken from *Alcyone* (Halcyon), a collection of poems which is D'Annunzio's masterpiece, intended to be part of a series of seven books dedicated to the Pleiades. Only four were completed: *Maia*, in 1903; *Electra*, with the aforementioned *Alcyone*, in 1904; and *Merope*, in 1912. The projected series was given a general title that in itself is the epitome of D'Annunzio's taste for the grandiose: *Laudi del Cielo, del Mare, della Terra, degli Eroi* (Praises of the Sky, of the Sea, of the Earth, of Heroes).

In 1921 D'Annunzio retired to his sumptuous villa on Lake Garda, which he baptized "Il Vittoriale degli Italiani" (Villa of the Italians' Victory) and which is today a national monument. There he lived in splendor until his death, surrounded by a unique collection of art objects and mementos of his war exploits.

Rain in the Pine Wood

> *Hush. On the edge*
> *Of the wood I do not hear*
> *Words which you call*
> *Human; but I hear*
> *Words which are newer*
> *Spoken by droplets and leaves*
> *Far away.*
> *Listen. Rain falls*
> *From the scattered clouds.*
> *Rain falls on the tamarisks*
> *Briny and parched,*
> *Rain falls on the pine trees*
> *Scaly and bristling,*
> *Rain falls on the myrtles—*
> *Divine,*

Su le ginestre fulgenti
Di fiori accolti,
Su i ginepri folti
Di coccole aulenti,
Piove su i nostri volti
Silvani,
Piove su le nostre mani
Ignude,
Su i nostri vestimenti
Leggieri,
Su i freschi pensieri
Che l'anima schiude
Novella,
Su la favola bella
Che ieri
T'illuse, che oggi m'illude,
O Ermione.

Odi? La pioggia cade
Su la solitaria
Verdura
Con un crepitìo che dura
E varia nell'aria
Secondo le fronde
Più rade, men rade.
Ascolta. Risponde
Al pianto il canto
Delle cicale
Che il pianto australe
Non impaura,
Nè il ciel cinerino.
E il pino
Ha un suono, e il mirto
Altro suono, e il ginepro
Altro ancora, stromenti
Diversi
Sotto innumerevoli dita.
E immersi
Noi siam nello spirto

On the broom-shrubs gleaming
With clustered flowers,
On the junipers thick
With fragrant berries,
Rain falls on our faces—
Sylvan,
Rain falls on our hands—
Naked,
On our clothes—
Light,
On the fresh thoughts
That our soul discloses—
Renewed,
On the lovely fable
That yesterday
Beguiled you, that beguiles me today,
O Hermione.

Do you hear? The rain is falling
On the solitary
Greenness
With a crackling that persists
And varies in the air
According to the foliage
Sparser, less sparse.
Listen. The weeping is answered
by the song
Of the cicadas
Which are not frightened
by the weeping of the south wind
Or the ashen sky.
And the pine tree
Has one sound, and the myrtle
Another sound, and the juniper
Yet another, instruments
Different
Under numberless fingers.
And we are
immersed in the spirit

Silvestre,
D'arborea vita viventi;
E il tuo volto ebro
È molle di pioggia
Come une foglia,
E le tue chiome
Auliscono come
Le chiare ginestre,
O creatura terrestre
Che hai nome
Ermione.

Ascolta, ascolta. L'accordo
Delle aeree cicale
A poco a poco
Più sordo
Si fa sotto il pianto
Che cresce;
Ma un canto vi si mesce
Più roco
Che di laggiù sale,
Dall'umida ombra remota.
Più sordo e più fioco
S'allenta, si spegne.
Sola una nota
Ancor trema, si spegne,
Risorge, trema, si spegne.
Non s'ode voce del mare.
Or s'ode su tutta la fronda
Crosciare
L'argentea pioggia
Che monda,
Il croscio che varia
Secondo la fronda
Più folta, men folta.
Ascolta.
La figlia dell'aria
È muta; ma la figlia
Del limo lontana,

Of the woodland,
Alive with arboreal life;
And your ecstatic face
Is soft with rain
As a leaf,
And your hair
Is fragrant like
The bright broom-flowers,
O earthly creature
Whose name is
Hermione.

Listen, listen. The harmony
Of the high-borne cicadas
Gradually becomes
fainter
beneath the weeping
That grows stronger;
But a song mingles with it—
Hoarser,
Rising from down there,
From the far damp shade.
Fainter and weaker
It slackens, fades away.
Only one note
Still trembles, fades away,
Rises again, trembles, fades away.
One hears no sea voice.
Now one hears upon all the foliage,
Pelting,
The silvery rain
That cleanses,
The pelting that varies
According to the foliage
Thicker, less thick.
Listen.
The daughter of the air
Is mute; but the daughter
Of the miry swamp, in the distance,

La rana,
Canta nell'ombra più fonda,
Chi sa dove, chi sa dove!
E piove su le tue ciglia,
Ermione.

Piove su le tue ciglia nere
Sì che par tu pianga
Ma di piacere; non bianca
Ma quasi fatta virente,
Par da scorza tu esca.
E tutta la vita è in noi fresca
Aulente,
Il cuor nel petto è come pesca
Intatta,
Tra le palpebre gli occhi
Son come polle tra l'erbe,
I denti negli alvèoli
Son come mandorle acerbe.
E andiam di fratta in fratta,
Or congiunti or disciolti
(E il verde vigor rude
Ci allaccia i mallèoli
C'intrica i ginocchi)
Chi sa dove, chi sa dove!
E piove su i nostri volti
Silvani,
Piove su le nostre mani
Ignude,
Su i nostri vestimenti
Leggieri,
Su i freschi pensieri
Che l'anima schiude
Novella,
Su la favola bella
Che ieri
M'illuse, che oggi t'illude,
O Ermione.

The frog,
Is singing in the deepest shade,
Who knows where, who knows where!
And rain falls on your lashes,
Hermione.

Rain falls on your black eyelashes
So that you seem to weep
But from pleasure; not white
But made almost green,
You seem to emerge from bark.
And within us all life is fresh,
Fragrant,
The heart in our breasts is like a peach
Untouched,
The eyes between the eyelids
Are like springs in the grass,
The teeth in their sockets
Are like bitter almonds.
And we go from thicket to thicket,
Now joined, now apart
(And the rough green vigor
Entwines our ankles,
Entangles our knees)
Who knows where, who knows where!
And rain falls on our faces—
Sylvan,
Rain falls on our hands—
Naked,
On our clothes—
Light,
On the fresh thoughts
That our soul discloses—
Renewed,
On the lovely fable
That yesterday
Beguiled me, that beguiles you today,
O Hermione.

GIUSEPPE UNGARETTI

(1888–1970)

A GROUP of Italian critics and writers, active during the years following the First World War, one day ominously proclaimed that poetry was dead, and that henceforth the only medium through which a poet might give lyrical expression to his emotions was prose. Apocalyptic statements of this kind are not new, but few predictions of doom have proved to be so completely wrong in recent times. Not only has poetry survived in twentieth-century Italy, but it has known a period of revival and greatness worthy of a tradition of poetic excellence going back more than seven centuries.

Three poets were outstanding in Italy during the first half of this century, three poets who were among the most distinguished literary representatives of the Western world: Giuseppe Ungaretti, Eugenio Montale, and Salvatore Quasimodo.

Ungaretti was the oldest of the three, and in a real sense the father of contemporary Italian poetry. Born in Alexandria, where his parents had settled after emigrating from Tuscany, he spent in Egypt the first twenty-four years of his life. This was a period that naturally had a great impact on the development of his poetry. One of the constantly recurring themes in his work—the desert—was the result of his direct contact with the Sahara. For Ungaretti, the desert means distance, light, freedom, and above all, dreams, mirages—the dreams and mirages of the nomad who becomes the symbol of the poet in his perennial wanderings in search of innocence, happiness, love.

In 1912 Ungaretti left Egypt to study at the Sorbonne. He remained in Paris until the outbreak of the First World War, during which he served as a private in the Italian infantry. In the trenches, during the lulls between battles, or at night in his tent, Ungaretti wrote a sort of diary on scraps of paper. Those scraps of paper were to become the pages of his first book of verse, *Il porto sepolto* (The Buried Port), which was published in 1916 and revolutionized Italian poetry. Most of the poems in this first volume were extremely short, the lines were not regular ones, there was no rhyme, no punctuation; the general versification represented a complete break with tradition. Yet those short poems had a freshness, an intensity, a regenerating strength that was uncannily captivating and moving. One such poem is "Veglia," our first selection. The date "Cima Quattro, il 23 dicembre 1915" gives this short lyric a precise setting (Peak Four, on the Alpine front) and time (two days before Christmas), helping the reader to grasp the atmosphere of the poem and to understand in particular the reference to those "letters full of love" mentioned in line 13.

Il porto sepolto was incorporated in 1919 into a larger collection of poems, *Allegria di naufragi* (Joy of Shipwrecks). This very title, echoing as it does the last line of Leopardi's "L'infinito" (see p. 104), indicates, as later poems revealed, that Ungaretti was then already seeking to get back into the mainstream of the great Italian lyric tradition and that he was rediscovering for himself the meters of the old masters, especially the hendecasyllablic line and the septenary. A glance at our second selection, "Senza più peso," from *Sentimento del tempo* (Sentiment of Time), will reveal its conventional appearance. No longer the short, hammered lines of poems like "Veglia," but a return to regular verse and to punctuation. Yet the distinct qualities characteristic of Ungaretti's work throughout his career—those qualities readily recognizable in "Veglia"—are still quite evident in "Senza più peso": a sparing use of words, a capacity to bring language to unusual heights of lyric tension, a power to create illuminating images.

"Senza più peso" was written in 1934. Ungaretti's son Antonietto—then four years old—was perhaps not extraneous to the basic theme of reconquered innocence in this poem, particularly in the striking image of "a God that might smile like a child" (line 1). Antonietto did provide the inspiration for several poems included in two books of collected verse published after *Sentimento del tempo*: *Il dolore*, 1947 (The Grief), and *Un grido e paesaggi*, 1952 (A Shout and Landscapes). Antonietto died at the age of nine in Brazil, and Ungaretti, who had gone to South America with his family to teach at the University of São Paulo, recorded in tragic, unforgettable lines the cosmic sense of bereavement he experienced with the loss of his son. "Tu ti spezzasti," the third selection, is one of these poems, certainly among the most powerful written by Ungaretti.

Upon his return from Brazil in 1942 Ungaretti was appointed Professor of Italian Literature at the University of Rome, a position he held until his retirement at the age of seventy-five. In 1962 he was elected by acclamation President of the European Community of Writers.

Veglia

Un'intera nottata
Buttato vicino
A un compagno
Massacrato
Con la sua bocca
Digrignata
Volta al plenilunio
Con la congestione
Delle sue mani
Penetrata
Nel mio silenzio
Ho scritto
Lettere piene d'amore

Non sono mai stato
Tanto
Attaccato alla vita

Cima Quattro, il 23 dicembre 1915

Senza più peso

Per un Iddio che rida come un bimbo,
Tanti gridi di passeri,
Tante danze nei rami,

Un'anima si fa senza più peso,
I prati hanno una tale tenerezza,
Tale pudore negli occhi rivive,

Le mani come foglie
S'incantano nell'aria . . .

Chi teme più, chi giudica?

124

Watch

An entire night
Thrown down beside
A comrade
Massacred
With his mouth
Snarling
Turned toward the full moon
With the congestion
Of his hands
Penetrating
Into my silence
I have written
Letters full of love

Never have I been
So
Tied to life

Peak Four, December 23, 1915

Weightless

For a God that might smile like a child,
So many cries of sparrows,
So much dancing in the branches,

A soul becomes weightless,
The meadows have such tenderness,
In the eyes such purity is reborn,

The hands like leaves
Are spellbound in the air . . .

Who now can fear, who can judge?

Tu ti spezzasti

1   I molti, immani, sparsi, grigi sassi
Frementi ancora alle segrete fionde
Di originarie fiamme soffocate
Od ai terrori di fiumane vergini
Ruinanti in implacabili carezze,
—Sopra l'abbaglio della sabbia rigidi
In un vuoto orizzonte, non rammenti?

E la recline, che s'apriva all'unico
Raccogliersi dell'ombra nella valle,
Araucaria, anelando ingigantita,
Volta nell'ardua selce d'erme fibre
Più delle altre dannate refrattaria,
Fresca la bocca di farfalle e d'erbe
Dove dalle radici si tagliava,
—Non la rammenti delirante muta
Sopra tre palmi d'un rotondo ciottolo
In un perfetto bilico
Magicamente apparsa?

Di ramo in ramo fiorrancino lieve,
Ebbri di meraviglia gli avidi occhi
Ne conquistavi la screziata cima,
Temerario, musico bimbo,
Solo per rivedere all'imo lucido
D'un fondo e quieto baratro di mare
Favolose testuggini
Ridestarsi fra le alghe.

Della natura estrema la tensione
E le subacquee pompe,
Funebri moniti.

You Were Shattered

1 The many, monstrous, scattered gray rocks
Still quivering from the secret slings
Of primordial flames now smothered,
Or from the terrors of virgin floods
Crashing down with implacable caresses;
—Over the dazzle of the sand, rigid [rocks]
Against an empty horizon, do you not remember?

And the reclining—opening out towards the only
Gathering of shade in the valley—
Araucaria, made gigantic by yearning,
Turned into lonely fibers of hard flint,
More refractory than any other doomed [plant],
Its mouth fresh with butterflies and grass
Where it was severed from its roots:
—Do you not remember [how], mutely delirious,
Upon three spans of a round pebble,
In perfect balance
[It] magically appeared?

From branch to branch, light firecrest,
Eager eyes drunk with wonder,
You conquered its variegated summit,
Daring, musical child,
Just to see once more in the luminous depth
Of a sunken and quiet chasm of the sea
Fabulous tortoises
Reawakening among the algae.

The extreme tension of nature
And the subaqueous pageants,
Funereal warnings.

2   Alzavi le braccia come ali
    E ridavi nascita al vento
    Correndo nel peso dell'aria immota.

    Nessuno mai vide posare
    Il tuo lieve piede di danza.

3   Grazia felice,
    Non avresti potuto non spezzarti
    In una cecità tanto indurita
    Tu semplice soffio e cristallo,

    Troppo umano lampo per l'empio,
    Selvoso, accanito, ronzante
    Ruggito d'un sole ignudo.

2   *You used to lift your arms like wings*
    And again give birth to the wind
    Running in the weight of the motionless air.

    No one ever saw at rest
    Your light foot, made for dancing.

3   *O happy grace,*
    You could not avoid being shattered
    In a blindness so obdurate,
    You, simple breath and crystal,

    Too human a flash for the profane,
    Jungle-wild, dogged, buzzing
    Roar of a naked sun.

EUGENIO MONTALE

(1896–1981)

EUGENIO MONTALE was born in Genoa. His father, a
successful importer, wanted his son to become a partner in
his firm. But Eugenio was not interested in business; he eventually
left his family, went to Florence, and for about ten years was
employed as director of an international lending library, a posi-
tion he lost shortly before the Second World War for being politi-
cally "undesirable," that is, for refusing to support the Fascist
regime. After 1945 he lived mostly in Milan, working as literary
editor and music critic for the influential newspaper *Corriere
della Sera*.

Montale gained international recognition as long ago as 1928,
when T. S. Eliot published one of his major compositions,
"Arsenio," in *The Criterion*. Nonetheless, Montale is not so widely
known among non-Italian readers as he deserves to be. Perhaps
this is partly because many of his poems are considered "diffi-
cult," and in fact their meaning—or at least the meaning of certain
telescoped images and private allusions—is sometimes obscure.
This accusation of obscurity, of writing what has been labeled
"hermetic poetry," has been brought not only against Montale,
but also against Ungaretti and Quasimodo. Montale replies that
no poet is hermetic or cryptic on purpose. He also insists that no
one would write poetry if his overriding aim were merely to be
understandable. For him the aim of poetry is always to express
something beyond the power of words to convey. And if a major
poet like Montale often finds it necessary to use an ellipsis or to
suppress any link between ideas and images in the effort to allow

the words to express their essential, deeper meanings, it will simply mean that we, as readers, will have to participate more actively, more imaginatively, to establish a communion of thought and feeling with the poet.

An especial tone of pessimism reverberates through Montale's work. Montale views life with sadness, at times even despair. His first book of verse, published in 1925, was titled *Ossi di seppia* (Cuttlefish Bones), and this title sums up his outlook on human existence as being at once filled with the forces of life yet desiccated. "I always felt in total disharmony with reality," he wrote in an autobiographical essay, "and *this* disharmony has been the source of my inspiration." In "Meriggiare pallido e assorto," our first selection, Montale compares life to a journey in the dazzling sun along a wall, the top of which is studded with pieces of broken glass. And in another poem, "Non chiederci la parola" (Do not ask of us the word), he warns his reader not to expect from him a magic formula capable of working miracles, of opening new worlds: for Montale, a poet can tell us only "what we are not, what we do not want."

Montale's pessimism also pervades "La casa dei doganieri" (The House of the Customs-Men), one of the most famous poems from the book *Le occasioni* (The Occasions; 1939), presented here as the second selection. The house referred to in the title (a look-out point against smugglers) reminds the poet of a lost love and of a past that cannot be recaptured.

Our third selection, "L'anguilla" (The Eel), from *La bufera e altro* (The Storm and Other Poems; 1956), strikes a very different note: not one of optimism, but certainly of faith in life's endurance and persistence. For no matter how bitter and frustrating man's existence, Montale knows that life cannot end, that it will continue to perpetuate itself with inscrutable and over-whelming power. The eel is the symbol of this self-perpetuating miracle of life: the eel—that is, woman, as the last line of this brilliant one-sentence poem suggests with its open question.

In June 1967 Montale received one of Italy's highest honors: in recognition of his literary and artistic merits, he was made Senator for life. The same month he was awarded an honorary degree in Letters by the University of Cambridge.

"*Meriggiare pallido e assorto*"

Meriggiare pallido e assorto
Presso un rovente muro d'orto,
Ascoltare tra i pruni e gli sterpi
Schiocchi di merli, frusci di serpi.

Nelle crepe del suolo o su la veccia
Spiar le file di rosse formiche
Ch'ora si rompono ed ora s'intrecciano
A sommo di minuscole biche.

Osservare tra frondi il palpitare
Lontano di scaglie di mare
Mentre si levano tremuli scricchi
Di cicale dai calvi picchi.

E andando nel sole che abbaglia
Sentire con triste meraviglia
Com'è tutta la vita e il suo travaglio
In questo seguitare una muraglia
Che ha in cima cocci aguzzi di bottiglia.

"To rest at noon, pale and absorbed"

To rest at noon, pale and absorbed,
Close to a scorching garden wall,
To hear among thornbushes and dry stalks
Clickings of blackbirds, rustling of snakes.

To seek out in the cracks of the ground
or on the vetch the files of red ants
Now breaking rank, now weaving together
Upon the tops of tiny mounds.

To observe through branches the distant
throbbing of scales of the sea
While tremulous screeches of cicadas
rise from the bald peaks.

And, walking in the dazzling sun,
To feel with sad amazement
How all of life and its travail
is in this following of a wall
Topped with jagged fragments of bottle.

La casa dei doganieri

Tu non ricordi la casa dei doganieri
Sul rialzo a strapiombo sulla scogliera:
Desolata t'attende dalla sera
In cui v'entrò lo sciame dei tuoi pensieri
E vi sostò irrequieto.

Libeccio sferza da anni le vecchie mura
E il suono del tuo riso non è più lieto:
La bussola va impazzita all'avventura
E il calcolo dei dadi più non torna.
Tu non ricordi; altro tempo frastorna
La tua memoria; un filo s'addipana.

Ne tengo ancora un capo; ma s'allontana
La casa e in cima al tetto la banderuola
Affumicata gira senza pietà.
Ne tengo un capo; ma tu resti sola
Nè qui rèspiri nell'oscurità.

Oh l'orizzonte in fuga, dove s'accende
Rara la luce della petroliera!
Il varco è qui? (Ripullula il frangente
Ancora sulla balza che scoscende . . .)
Tu non ricordi la casa di questa
Mia sera. Ed io non so chi va e chi resta.

The House of the Customs-Men

You do not remember the house of the customs-men
On the edge of the steep cliff overhanging the reef:
Desolate it has been waiting for you since that evening
When the swarm of your thoughts entered it,
And paused there, restless.

The south wind has battered the old walls for years
And the sound of your laughter is no longer gay:
The compass veers crazily at random
And the numbers on the dice no longer tally.
You do not remember; another time confuses
Your memory; and a thread is wound.

I still hold an end of it; but the house
recedes, and on top of the roof the weathervane,
Blackened by smoke, spins pitilessly.
I hold an end of it; but you remain alone
And do not breathe here in the darkness.

Oh the retreating horizon, where
the tanker's light rarely flares!
Is this the way through? (The breakers seethe
As ever at the plunging cliffs . . .)
You do not remember the house of this
My evening. And I do not know who is going and who remains.

L'anguilla

L'anguilla, la sirena
Dei mari freddi che lascia il Baltico
Per giungere ai nostri mari,
Ai nostri estuari, ai fiumi
Che risale in profondo, sotto la piena avversa,
Di ramo in ramo e poi
Di capello in capello, assottigliati,
Sempre più addentro, sempre più nel cuore
Del macigno, filtrando
Tra gorielli di melma finchè un giorno
Una luce scoccata dai castagni
Ne accende il guizzo in pozze d'acquamorta,
Nei fossi che declinano
Dai balzi d'Appennino alla Romagna;
L'anguilla, torcia, frusta,
Freccia d'Amore in terra
Che solo i nostri botri o i disseccati
Ruscelli pirenaici riconducono
A paradisi di fecondazione;
L'anima verde che cerca
Vita là dove solo
Morde l'arsura e la desolazione,
La scintilla che dice
Tutto comincia quando tutto pare
Incarbonirsi, bronco seppellito;
L'iride breve, gemella
Di quella che incastonano i tuoi cigli
E fai brillare intatta in mezzo ai figli
Dell'uomo, immersi nel tuo fango, puoi tu
Non crederla sorella?

The Eel

The eel, the siren
Of the frigid seas that abandons the Baltic
To join our seas,
Our estuaries, the rivers
Which it ascends in their depths, against the
    opposing flood,
From branch to branch, and then
From hair to hair, as they become thinner,
Ever more inward, ever more into the heart
Of the mountain rock, straining
Through runnels of slime until one day
A light shot from the chestnut trees
Ignites its streak in pools of dead water,
In the channels that descend
From the Apennine ridges toward the Romagna;
The eel, torch, lash,
Arrow of Love on earth
That only our gullies or the dried-out
Streams of the Pyrenees bring back
To paradises of fecundation;
The green soul that is seeking
Life there where only
Drought and desolation gnaw,
The spark that is saying
All begins when all appears
Burnt to carbon, a buried stump;
The brief rainbow, twin
To the one you set like a jewel between your lashes
And keep aglow inviolate among the sons
Of man, steeped in your mire, can you
Not believe it your sister?

SALVATORE QUASIMODO

(1901–1968)

THE last poet in this anthology, Salvatore Quasimodo, became world-famous when he won the Nobel Prize for Literature in 1959. Born in the small Sicilian town of Modica near Syracuse, the son of a railroad employee, he studied at technical schools to become an engineer, but was forced to leave because of financial difficulties. In his twenties, while working in the Civil Engineering Bureau of the state railroad, he began studying Latin and Greek on his own. He later made a number of fine verse translations from these two languages into Italian. In the mid-thirties Quasimodo settled in Milan, spent the war years there, and became Professor of Italian Literature at the Milan Conservatory of Music—a position he held until his death.

In the opening passages of his *Discourse on Poetry*, published in 1956, Quasimodo remarked that poetry undergoes a basic change during and after a war, since war alters the moral life of a people and fosters a greater need for truth than is felt in normal times. Whether or not one agrees with this view, one must admit that it applies very neatly to Quasimodo's own literary career, which is divided into two clearly distinct periods, with World War Two as the line of demarcation.

Quasimodo's early books bear such titles as *Acque e terre* (Waters and Lands), *Oboe sommerso* (Submerged Oboe), *Odore d'eucalipto* (Fragrance of Eucalyptus), *Erato e Apollion* (Erato and Apollion)—which suggest that the poet was chiefly concerned with nature (especially the nature of his native Sicily), with beauty, with love. His main influences were lyric poets: the Greek and

Latin writers from Homer to Virgil and Catullus whose works he was then translating, Leopardi, and especially his contemporaries—"hermetic" poets such as Ungaretti and Montale. "Antico inverno," our first selection, is one of the most representative examples of this early period—an exquisite lyric incantation of love and cyclic change, of death and rebirth. The various images the poem evokes seem to float freely, yet form a sequence of their own.

In 1942 Quasimodo collected all his poems and issued them in a book called *Ed è subito sera* (And Suddenly It Is Evening). The title, from an early poem, became in its new context a symbolic statement of the change in Quasimodo's work—a change, as he himself explained later, caused by the impact of the war and by the realization that a poet could no longer concern himself with idyllic verse and lyric enigmas.

The books that followed all reflect this change. In 1946 he issued a volume called *Con il piede straniero sopra il cuore* (With the Alien Foot upon Our Heart), written during the occupation of Italy. In a few years these poems were joined with others of a similar cast in a volume, *Giorno dopo giorno* (Day after Day), which stood as a kind of diary of the tragedy of the war years. And then, in his third post-war book, Quasimodo with its very title reinforced his changed attitude. It is called *La vita non è sogno* (Life Is Not a Dream), and the poems and the author's statements about poetry combine to insist that the poet's position in society cannot be passive and dreamlike: in times such as ours, poetry cannot consist of abstract modulations of one's feelings.

And so we had a new poet in Quasimodo—he was a *poète engagé*, a poet committed to voicing, and seeking to solve, the social problems of his time. A poet, we may say, of social awareness and concern. It was to the *poète engagé* that the Swedish Academy awarded its prize in 1959, for the citation commended Quasimodo for expressing in his poetry "the tragic experience of life in our time." Probably the most poignant of such poems is the one that appears as our second selection. It is called "Uomo del mio tempo" and is an indictment of war, all wars. Quasimodo was in Milan during that terrible week in August 1943 when the city suffered four aerial bombardments by hundreds of planes. It is certainly not by coincidence that one of the first images of the poem portrays man as an aviator sitting in the cockpit of a combat plane. "Uomo del mio tempo" is permeated with an atmosphere of horror, death, and cruelty. The poet exhorts the younger generation to forget their fathers—that is, to repudiate their forebears and start a new era in which war can be forgotten.

Antico inverno

Desiderio delle tue mani chiare
Nella penombra della fiamma:
Sapevano di rovere e di rose;
Di morte. Antico inverno.

Cercavano il miglio gli uccelli
Ed erano subito di neve;
Così le parole:
Un pò di sole, una raggera d'angelo,
E poi la nebbia; e gli alberi,
E noi fatti d'aria al mattino.

Uomo del mio tempo

Sei ancora quello della pietra e della fionda,
Uomo del mio tempo. Eri nella carlinga,
Con le ali maligne, le meridiane di morte,
—T'ho visto—dentro il carro di fuoco, alle forche,
Alle ruote di tortura. T'ho visto: eri tu,
Con la tua scienza esatta persuasa allo sterminio,
Senza amore, senza Cristo. Hai ucciso ancora,
Come sempre, come uccisero i padri, come uccisero
Gli animali che ti videro per la prima volta.
E questo sangue odora come nel giorno
Quando il fratello disse all'altro fratello:
"Andiamo ai campi." E quell'eco fredda, tenace,
È giunta fino a te, dentro la tua giornata.
Dimenticate, o figli, le nuvole di sangue
Salite dalla terra, dimenticate i padri:
Le loro tombe affondano nella cenere,
Gli uccelli neri, il vento, coprono il loro cuore.

Ancient Winter

Desire of your hands white
In the penumbra of the flame:
They had the fragrance of oak and of roses;
Of death. Ancient winter.

The birds were looking for millet
And were suddenly of snow;
So with words:
A bit of sun, an angel's halo,
And then the mist; and the trees,
And ourselves made of air in the morning.

Man of My Time

You are still the one with the stone and the sling,
Man of my time. You were in the cockpit,
With the malevolent wings, the meridians of death,
—I have seen you—in the chariot of fire, at the gallows,
At the wheels of torture. I have seen you: it was you,
With your exact science set on extermination,
Without love, without Christ. You have killed again,
As always, as your fathers killed,
as the animals killed that saw you for the first time.
And this blood smells as on the day
When one brother told the other brother:
"Let us go into the fields." And that echo, chill, tenacious,
Has reached down to you, within your day.
Forget, O sons, the clouds of blood
Risen from the earth, forget your fathers:
Their tombs sink down in ashes,
Black birds, the wind, cover their heart.

PICTURE SOURCES AND CREDITS

SAN FRANCESCO D'ASSISI (p. 6): detail of fresco by Simone Martini in the Lower Church at Assisi.

LA COMPIUTA DONZELLA (p. 12): no known portrait; illustration shows panorama of Florence in the fourteenth century, a detail from the fresco "The Madonna of Mercy" in the Loggia del Bigallo, Florence; *Alinari photo.*

GUIDO CAVALCANTI (p. 16): no authentic portrait found; illustration shows a *canzone* of Cavalcanti in Manuscript 1094 of the Biblioteca Riccardiana, Florence; *photo courtesy of Biblioteca Riccardiana.*

CECCO ANGIOLIERI (p. 20): no known portrait; illustration shows the sonnet "S'i' fosse foco, arderei 'l mondo" in Manuscript 1103 of the Biblioteca Riccardiana, Florence; *photo courtesy of Biblioteca Riccardiana.*

DANTE ALIGHIERI (p. 24): detail of fresco by Giotto, in the Bargello, Florence.

FRANCESCO PETRARCA (p. 34): manuscript miniature, about 1400,

GIOVANNI BOCCACCIO (p. 40): illumination from a fourteenth-century manuscript (Codex 38) in the Bibliothèque Nationale, Paris.

FRANCO SACCHETTI (p. 46): no authentic portrait found; illustration shows the *caccia* "Passando con pensier per un boschetto" in the autograph manuscript of Sacchetti's *Rime* (MS Ashburnhamiano 574) in the Biblioteca Medicea Laurenziana, Florence; *photo courtesy of Biblioteca Medicea Laurenziana.*

LORENZO DE' MEDICI (p. 52): painting by Giorgio Vasari in the Uffizi, Florence.

ANGELO POLIZIANO (p. 60): detail of fresco by Domenico Ghirlandaio in the Chiesa di S. Trinita, Florence; *Alinari photo.*

LUDOVICO ARIOSTO (p. 66): engraving by Enea Vico of Parma.

MICHELANGELO BUONARROTI (p. 74): anonymous engraving.

FRANCESCO BERNI (p. 80): engraving by G. Mari after a portrait by G. Longhi.

TORQUATO TASSO (p. 84): painting by A. Allori in the Uffizi, Florence.

GIAMBATTISTA MARINO (p. 92): engraving by F. Valerio; photo courtesy of Biblioteca Nazionale Marciana, Venice.

UGO FOSCOLO (p. 96): anonymous engraving.

GIACOMO LEOPARDI (p. 102): pencil portrait from life by Lolli, 1826.

GABRIELE D'ANNUNZIO (p. 110): from a photograph.

GIUSEPPE UNGARETTI (p. 120), EUGENIO MONTALE (p. 130) and SALVATORE QUASIMODO (p. 140): *photos courtesy of Arnoldo Mondadori, Editore, Milan.*

A CATALOG OF SELECTED
DOVER BOOKS
IN ALL FIELDS OF INTEREST

A CATALOG OF SELECTED DOVER BOOKS IN ALL FIELDS OF INTEREST

DRAWINGS OF REMBRANDT, edited by Seymour Slive. Updated Lippmann, Hofstede de Groot edition, with definitive scholarly apparatus. All portraits, biblical sketches, landscapes, nudes. Oriental figures, classical studies, together with selection of work by followers. 550 illustrations. Total of 630pp. 9⅛ × 12¼.
21485-0, 21486-9 Pa., Two-vol. set $29.90

GHOST AND HORROR STORIES OF AMBROSE BIERCE, Ambrose Bierce. 24 tales vividly imagined, strangely prophetic, and decades ahead of their time in technical skill: "The Damned Thing," "An Inhabitant of Carcosa," "The Eyes of the Panther," "Moxon's Master," and 20 more. 199pp. 5⅜ × 8½. 20767-6 Pa. $3.95

ETHICAL WRITINGS OF MAIMONIDES, Maimonides. Most significant ethical works of great medieval sage, newly translated for utmost precision, readability. Laws Concerning Character Traits, Eight Chapters, more. 192pp. 5⅜ × 8½.
24522-5 Pa. $4.50

THE EXPLORATION OF THE COLORADO RIVER AND ITS CANYONS, J. W. Powell. Full text of Powell's 1,000-mile expedition down the fabled Colorado in 1869. Superb account of terrain, geology, vegetation, Indians, famine, mutiny, treacherous rapids, mighty canyons, during exploration of last unknown part of continental U.S. 400pp. 5⅜ × 8½. 20094-9 Pa. $7.95

HISTORY OF PHILOSOPHY, Julián Marías. Clearest one-volume history on the market. Every major philosopher and dozens of others, to Existentialism and later. 505pp. 5⅜ × 8½. 21739-6 Pa. $9.95

ALL ABOUT LIGHTNING, Martin A. Uman. Highly readable non-technical survey of nature and causes of lightning, thunderstorms, ball lightning, St. Elmo's Fire, much more. Illustrated. 192pp. 5⅜ × 8½. 25237-X Pa. $5.95

SAILING ALONE AROUND THE WORLD, Captain Joshua Slocum. First man to sail around the world, alone, in small boat. One of great feats of seamanship told in delightful manner. 67 illustrations. 294pp. 5⅜ × 8½. 20326-3 Pa. $4.95

LETTERS AND NOTES ON THE MANNERS, CUSTOMS AND CONDITIONS OF THE NORTH AMERICAN INDIANS, George Catlin. Classic account of life among Plains Indians: ceremonies, hunt, warfare, etc. 312 plates. 572pp. of text. 6⅛ × 9¼. 22118-0, 22119-9, Pa. Two-vol. set $17.90

ALASKA: The Harriman Expedition, 1899, John Burroughs, John Muir, et al. Informative, engrossing accounts of two-month, 9,000-mile expedition. Native peoples, wildlife, forests, geography, salmon industry, glaciers, more. Profusely illustrated. 240 black-and-white line drawings. 124 black-and-white photographs. 3 maps. Index. 576pp. 5⅜ × 8½. 25109-8 Pa. $11.95

THE BOOK OF BEASTS: Being a Translation from a Latin Bestiary of the Twelfth Century, T. H. White. Wonderful catalog real and fanciful beasts: manticore, griffin, phoenix, amphivius, jaculus, many more. White's witty erudite commentary on scientific, historical aspects. Fascinating glimpse of medieval mind. Illustrated. 296pp. 5⅜ × 8¼. (Available in U.S. only)　　　24609-4 Pa. $6.95

FRANK LLOYD WRIGHT: ARCHITECTURE AND NATURE With 160 Illustrations, Donald Hoffmann. Profusely illustrated study of influence of nature—especially prairie—on Wright's designs for Fallingwater, Robie House, Guggenheim Museum, other masterpieces. 96pp. 9¼ × 10¾.　　　25098-9 Pa. $7.95

FRANK LLOYD WRIGHT'S FALLINGWATER, Donald Hoffmann. Wright's famous waterfall house: planning and construction of organic idea. History of site, owners, Wright's personal involvement. Photographs of various stages of building. Preface by Edgar Kaufmann, Jr. 100 illustrations. 112pp. 9¼ × 10.

23671-4 Pa. $8.95

YEARS WITH FRANK LLOYD WRIGHT: Apprentice to Genius, Edgar Tafel. Insightful memoir by a former apprentice presents a revealing portrait of Wright the man, the inspired teacher, the greatest American architect. 372 black-and-white illustrations. Preface. Index. vi + 228pp. 8¼ × 11.　　　24801-1 Pa. $10.95

THE STORY OF KING ARTHUR AND HIS KNIGHTS, Howard Pyle. Enchanting version of King Arthur fable has delighted generations with imaginative narratives of exciting adventures and unforgettable illustrations by the author. 41 illustrations. xviii + 313pp. 6⅛ × 9¼.　　　21445-1 Pa. $6.95

THE GODS OF THE EGYPTIANS, E. A. Wallis Budge. Thorough coverage of numerous gods of ancient Egypt by foremost Egyptologist. Information on evolution of cults, rites and gods; the cult of Osiris; the Book of the Dead and its rites; the sacred animals and birds; Heaven and Hell; and more. 956pp. 6⅛ × 9¼.

22055-9, 22056-7 Pa., Two-vol. set $21.90

A THEOLOGICO-POLITICAL TREATISE, Benedict Spinoza. Also contains unfinished *Political Treatise*. Great classic on religious liberty, theory of government on common consent. R. Elwes translation. Total of 421pp. 5⅜ × 8½.

20249-6 Pa. $6.95

INCIDENTS OF TRAVEL IN CENTRAL AMERICA, CHIAPAS, AND YUCATAN, John L. Stephens. Almost single-handed discovery of Maya culture; exploration of ruined cities, monuments, temples; customs of Indians. 115 drawings. 892pp. 5⅜ × 8½.　　　22404-X, 22405-8 Pa., Two-vol. set $15.90

LOS CAPRICHOS, Francisco Goya. 80 plates of wild, grotesque monsters and caricatures. Prado manuscript included. 183pp. 6⅛ × 9⅜.　　　22384-1 Pa. $5.95

AUTOBIOGRAPHY: The Story of My Experiments with Truth, Mohandas K. Gandhi. Not hagiography, but Gandhi in his own words. Boyhood, legal studies, purification, the growth of the Satyagraha (nonviolent protest) movement. Critical, inspiring work of the man who freed India. 480pp. 5⅜ × 8½. (Available in U.S. only)

24593-4 Pa. $6.95

ILLUSTRATED DICTIONARY OF HISTORIC ARCHITECTURE, edited by Cyril M. Harris. Extraordinary compendium of clear, concise definitions for over 5,000 important architectural terms complemented by over 2,000 line drawings. Covers full spectrum of architecture from ancient ruins to 20th-century Modernism. Preface. 592pp. 7½ × 9⅝. 24444-X Pa. $15.95

THE NIGHT BEFORE CHRISTMAS, Clement Moore. Full text, and woodcuts from original 1848 book. Also critical, historical material. 19 illustrations. 40pp. 4⅝ × 6. 22797-9 Pa. $2.50

THE LESSON OF JAPANESE ARCHITECTURE: 165 Photographs, Jiro Harada. Memorable gallery of 165 photographs taken in the 1930's of exquisite Japanese homes of the well-to-do and historic buildings. 13 line diagrams. 192pp. 8⅜ × 11¼. 24778-3 Pa. $10.95

THE AUTOBIOGRAPHY OF CHARLES DARWIN AND SELECTED LETTERS, edited by Francis Darwin. The fascinating life of eccentric genius composed of an intimate memoir by Darwin (intended for his children); commentary by his son, Francis; hundreds of fragments from notebooks, journals, papers; and letters to and from Lyell, Hooker, Huxley, Wallace and Henslow. xi + 365pp. 5⅜ × 8. 20479-0 Pa. $6.95

WONDERS OF THE SKY: Observing Rainbows, Comets, Eclipses, the Stars and Other Phenomena, Fred Schaaf. Charming, easy-to-read poetic guide to all manner of celestial events visible to the naked eye. Mock suns, glories, Belt of Venus, more. Illustrated. 299pp. 5¼ × 8¼. 24402-4 Pa. $7.95

BURNHAM'S CELESTIAL HANDBOOK, Robert Burnham, Jr. Thorough guide to the stars beyond our solar system. Exhaustive treatment. Alphabetical by constellation: Andromeda to Cetus in Vol. 1; Chamaeleon to Orion in Vol. 2; and Pavo to Vulpecula in Vol. 3. Hundreds of illustrations. Index in Vol. 3. 2,000pp. 6⅛ × 9¼. 23567-X, 23568-8, 23673-0 Pa., Three-vol. set $41.85

STAR NAMES: Their Lore and Meaning, Richard Hinckley Allen. Fascinating history of names various cultures have given to constellations and literary and folkloristic uses that have been made of stars. Indexes to subjects. Arabic and Greek names. Biblical references. Bibliography. 563pp. 5⅜ × 8½. 21079-0 Pa. $8.95

THIRTY YEARS THAT SHOOK PHYSICS: The Story of Quantum Theory, George Gamow. Lucid, accessible introduction to influential theory of energy and matter. Careful explanations of Dirac's anti-particles, Bohr's model of the atom, much more. 12 plates. Numerous drawings. 240pp. 5⅜ × 8½. 24895-X Pa. $5.95

CHINESE DOMESTIC FURNITURE IN PHOTOGRAPHS AND MEASURED DRAWINGS, Gustav Ecke. A rare volume, now affordably priced for antique collectors, furniture buffs and art historians. Detailed review of styles ranging from early Shang to late Ming. Unabridged republication. 161 black-and-white drawings, photos. Total of 224pp. 8⅜ × 11¼. (Available in U.S. only) 25171-3 Pa. $13.95

VINCENT VAN GOGH: A Biography, Julius Meier-Graefe. Dynamic, penetrating study of artist's life, relationship with brother, Theo, painting techniques, travels, more. Readable, engrossing. 160pp. 5⅜ × 8½. (Available in U.S. only) 25253-1 Pa. $4.95

HOW TO WRITE, Gertrude Stein. Gertrude Stein claimed anyone could understand her unconventional writing—here are clues to help. Fascinating improvisations, language experiments, explanations illuminate Stein's craft and the art of writing. Total of 414pp. 4⅝ × 6⅜. 23144-5 Pa. $6.95

ADVENTURES AT SEA IN THE GREAT AGE OF SAIL: Five Firsthand Narratives, edited by Elliot Snow. Rare true accounts of exploration, whaling, shipwreck, fierce natives, trade, shipboard life, more. 33 illustrations. Introduction. 353pp. 5⅜ × 8½. 25177-2 Pa. $8.95

THE HERBAL OR GENERAL HISTORY OF PLANTS, John Gerard. Classic descriptions of about 2,850 plants—with over 2,700 illustrations—includes Latin and English names, physical descriptions, varieties, time and place of growth, more. 2,706 illustrations. xlv + 1,678pp. 8½ × 12¼. 23147-X Cloth. $75.00

DOROTHY AND THE WIZARD IN OZ, L. Frank Baum. Dorothy and the Wizard visit the center of the Earth, where people are vegetables, glass houses grow and Oz characters reappear. Classic sequel to *Wizard of Oz.* 256pp. 5⅜ × 8.
24714-7 Pa. $5.95

SONGS OF EXPERIENCE: Facsimile Reproduction with 26 Plates in Full Color, William Blake. This facsimile of Blake's original "Illuminated Book" reproduces 26 full-color plates from a rare 1826 edition. Includes "The Tyger," "London," "Holy Thursday," and other immortal poems. 26 color plates. Printed text of poems. 48pp. 5¼ × 7. 24636-1 Pa. $3.50

SONGS OF INNOCENCE, William Blake. The first and most popular of Blake's famous "Illuminated Books," in a facsimile edition reproducing all 31 brightly colored plates. Additional printed text of each poem. 64pp. 5¼ × 7.
22764-2 Pa. $3.50

PRECIOUS STONES, Max Bauer. Classic, thorough study of diamonds, rubies, emeralds, garnets, etc.: physical character, occurrence, properties, use, similar topics. 20 plates, 8 in color. 94 figures. 659pp. 6⅛ × 9¼.
21910-0, 21911-9 Pa., Two-vol. set $15.90

ENCYCLOPEDIA OF VICTORIAN NEEDLEWORK, S. F. A. Caulfeild and Blanche Saward. Full, precise descriptions of stitches, techniques for dozens of needlecrafts—most exhaustive reference of its kind. Over 800 figures. Total of 679pp. 8⅛ × 11. Two volumes. Vol. 1 22800-2 Pa. $11.95
Vol. 2 22801-0 Pa. $11.95

THE MARVELOUS LAND OF OZ, L. Frank Baum. Second Oz book, the Scarecrow and Tin Woodman are back with hero named Tip, Oz magic. 136 illustrations. 287pp. 5⅜ × 8½. 20692-0 Pa. $5.95

WILD FOWL DECOYS, Joel Barber. Basic book on the subject, by foremost authority and collector. Reveals history of decoy making and rigging, place in American culture, different kinds of decoys, how to make them, and how to use them. 140 plates. 156pp. 7⅞ × 10¾. 20011-6 Pa. $8.95

HISTORY OF LACE, Mrs. Bury Palliser. Definitive, profusely illustrated chronicle of lace from earliest times to late 19th century. Laces of Italy, Greece, England, France, Belgium, etc. Landmark of needlework scholarship. 266 illustrations. 672pp. 6⅛ × 9¼. 24742-2 Pa. $14.95

ILLUSTRATED GUIDE TO SHAKER FURNITURE, Robert Meader. All furniture and appurtenances, with much on unknown local styles. 235 photos. 146pp. 9 × 12. 22819-3 Pa. $8.95

WHALE SHIPS AND WHALING: A Pictorial Survey, George Francis Dow. Over 200 vintage engravings, drawings, photographs of barks, brigs, cutters, other vessels. Also harpoons, lances, whaling guns, many other artifacts. Comprehensive text by foremost authority. 207 black-and-white illustrations. 288pp. 6 × 9.
24808-9 Pa. $8.95

THE BERTRAMS, Anthony Trollope. Powerful portrayal of blind self-will and thwarted ambition includes one of Trollope's most heartrending love stories. 497pp. 5⅜ × 8½. 25119-5 Pa. $9.95

ADVENTURES WITH A HAND LENS, Richard Headstrom. Clearly written guide to observing and studying flowers and grasses, fish scales, moth and insect wings, egg cases, buds, feathers, seeds, leaf scars, moss, molds, ferns, common crystals, etc.—all with an ordinary, inexpensive magnifying glass. 209 exact line drawings aid in your discoveries. 220pp. 5⅜ × 8½. 23330-8 Pa. $4.95

RODIN ON ART AND ARTISTS, Auguste Rodin. Great sculptor's candid, wide-ranging comments on meaning of art; great artists; relation of sculpture to poetry, painting, music; philosophy of life, more. 76 superb black-and-white illustrations of Rodin's sculpture, drawings and prints. 119pp. 8⅜ × 11¼. 24487-3 Pa. $7.95

FIFTY CLASSIC FRENCH FILMS, 1912–1982: A Pictorial Record, Anthony Slide. Memorable stills from Grand Illusion, Beauty and the Beast, Hiroshima, Mon Amour, many more. Credits, plot synopses, reviews, etc. 160pp. 8¼ × 11.
25256-6 Pa. $11.95

THE PRINCIPLES OF PSYCHOLOGY, William James. Famous long course complete, unabridged. Stream of thought, time perception, memory, experimental methods; great work decades ahead of its time. 94 figures. 1,391pp. 5⅜ × 8½.
20381-6, 20382-4 Pa., Two-vol. set $23.90

BODIES IN A BOOKSHOP, R. T. Campbell. Challenging mystery of blackmail and murder with ingenious plot and superbly drawn characters. In the best tradition of British suspense fiction. 192pp. 5⅜ × 8½. 24720-1 Pa. $3.95

CALLAS: PORTRAIT OF A PRIMA DONNA, George Jellinek. Renowned commentator on the musical scene chronicles incredible career and life of the most controversial, fascinating, influential operatic personality of our time. 64 black-and-white photographs. 416pp. 5⅜ × 8¼. 25047-4 Pa. $8.95

GEOMETRY, RELATIVITY AND THE FOURTH DIMENSION, Rudolph Rucker. Exposition of fourth dimension, concepts of relativity as Flatland characters continue adventures. Popular, easily followed yet accurate, profound. 141 illustrations. 133pp. 5⅜ × 8½. 23400-2 Pa. $4.95

HOUSEHOLD STORIES BY THE BROTHERS GRIMM, with pictures by Walter Crane. 53 classic stories—Rumpelstiltskin, Rapunzel, Hansel and Gretel, the Fisherman and his Wife, Snow White, Tom Thumb, Sleeping Beauty, Cinderella, and so much more—lavishly illustrated with original 19th century drawings. 114 illustrations. x + 269pp. 5⅜ × 8½. 21080-4 Pa. $4.95

SUNDIALS, Albert Waugh. Far and away the best, most thorough coverage of ideas, mathematics concerned, types, construction, adjusting anywhere. Over 100 illustrations. 230pp. 5⅜ × 8½. 22947-5 Pa. $4.95

PICTURE HISTORY OF THE NORMANDIE: With 190 Illustrations, Frank O. Braynard. Full story of legendary French ocean liner: Art Deco interiors, design innovations, furnishings, celebrities, maiden voyage, tragic fire, much more. Extensive text. 144pp. 8⅞ × 11¾. 25257-4 Pa. $10.95

THE FIRST AMERICAN COOKBOOK: A Facsimile of "American Cookery," 1796, Amelia Simmons. Facsimile of the first American-written cookbook published in the United States contains authentic recipes for colonial favorites—pumpkin pudding, winter squash pudding, spruce beer, Indian slapjacks, and more. Introductory Essay and Glossary of colonial cooking terms. 80pp. 5⅜ × 8½. 24710-4 Pa. $3.50

101 PUZZLES IN THOUGHT AND LOGIC, C. R. Wylie, Jr. Solve murders and robberies, find out which fishermen are liars, how a blind man could possibly identify a color—purely by your own reasoning! 107pp. 5⅜ × 8½. 20367-0 Pa. $2.50

THE BOOK OF WORLD-FAMOUS MUSIC—CLASSICAL, POPULAR AND FOLK, James J. Fuld. Revised and enlarged republication of landmark work in musico-bibliography. Full information about nearly 1,000 songs and compositions including first lines of music and lyrics. New supplement. Index. 800pp. 5⅜ × 8¼. 24857-7 Pa. $15.95

ANTHROPOLOGY AND MODERN LIFE, Franz Boas. Great anthropologist's classic treatise on race and culture. Introduction by Ruth Bunzel. Only inexpensive paperback edition. 255pp. 5⅜ × 8½. 25245-0 Pa. $6.95

THE TALE OF PETER RABBIT, Beatrix Potter. The inimitable Peter's terrifying adventure in Mr. McGregor's garden, with all 27 wonderful, full-color Potter illustrations. 55pp. 4¼ × 5½. (Available in U.S. only) 22827-4 Pa. $1.75

THREE PROPHETIC SCIENCE FICTION NOVELS, H. G. Wells. *When the Sleeper Wakes, A Story of the Days to Come* and *The Time Machine* (full version). 335pp. 5⅜ × 8½. (Available in U.S. only) 20605-X Pa. $6.95

APICIUS COOKERY AND DINING IN IMPERIAL ROME, edited and translated by Joseph Dommers Vehling. Oldest known cookbook in existence offers readers a clear picture of what foods Romans ate, how they prepared them, etc. 49 illustrations. 301pp. 6⅛ × 9¼. 23563-7 Pa. $7.95

SHAKESPEARE LEXICON AND QUOTATION DICTIONARY, Alexander Schmidt. Full definitions, locations, shades of meaning of every word in plays and poems. More than 50,000 exact quotations. 1,485pp. 6½ × 9¼. 22726-X, 22727-8 Pa., Two-vol. set $29.90

THE WORLD'S GREAT SPEECHES, edited by Lewis Copeland and Lawrence W. Lamm. Vast collection of 278 speeches from Greeks to 1970. Powerful and effective models; unique look at history. 842pp. 5⅜ × 8½. 20468-5 Pa. $11.95

THE BLUE FAIRY BOOK, Andrew Lang. The first, most famous collection, with many familiar tales: Little Red Riding Hood, Aladdin and the Wonderful Lamp, Puss in Boots, Sleeping Beauty, Hansel and Gretel, Rumpelstiltskin; 37 in all. 138 illustrations. 390pp. 5⅜ × 8½. 21437-0 Pa. $6.95

THE STORY OF THE CHAMPIONS OF THE ROUND TABLE, Howard Pyle. Sir Launcelot, Sir Tristram and Sir Percival in spirited adventures of love and triumph retold in Pyle's inimitable style. 50 drawings, 31 full-page. xviii + 329pp. 6½ × 9¼. 21883-X Pa. $7.95

AUDUBON AND HIS JOURNALS, Maria Audubon. Unmatched two-volume portrait of the great artist, naturalist and author contains his journals, an excellent biography by his granddaughter, expert annotations by the noted ornithologist, Dr. Elliott Coues, and 37 superb illustrations. Total of 1,200pp. 5⅜ × 8.
Vol. I 25143-8 Pa. $8.95
Vol. II 25144-6 Pa. $8.95

GREAT DINOSAUR HUNTERS AND THEIR DISCOVERIES, Edwin H. Colbert. Fascinating, lavishly illustrated chronicle of dinosaur research, 1820's to 1960. Achievements of Cope, Marsh, Brown, Buckland, Mantell, Huxley, many others. 384pp. 5¼ × 8¼. 24701-5 Pa. $7.95

THE TASTEMAKERS, Russell Lynes. Informal, illustrated social history of American taste 1850's–1950's. First popularized categories Highbrow, Lowbrow, Middlebrow. 129 illustrations. New (1979) afterword. 384pp. 6 × 9.
23993-4 Pa. $8.95

DOUBLE CROSS PURPOSES, Ronald A. Knox. A treasure hunt in the Scottish Highlands, an old map, unidentified corpse, surprise discoveries keep reader guessing in this cleverly intricate tale of financial skullduggery. 2 black-and-white maps. 320pp. 5⅜ × 8½. (Available in U.S. only) 25032-6 Pa. $6.95

AUTHENTIC VICTORIAN DECORATION AND ORNAMENTATION IN FULL COLOR: 46 Plates from "Studies in Design," Christopher Dresser. Superb full-color lithographs reproduced from rare original portfolio of a major Victorian designer. 48pp. 9¼ × 12¼. 25083-0 Pa. $7.95

PRIMITIVE ART, Franz Boas. Remains the best text ever prepared on subject, thoroughly discussing Indian, African, Asian, Australian, and, especially, Northern American primitive art. Over 950 illustrations show ceramics, masks, totem poles, weapons, textiles, paintings, much more. 376pp. 5⅜ × 8. 20025-6 Pa. $7.95

SIDELIGHTS ON RELATIVITY, Albert Einstein. Unabridged republication of two lectures delivered by the great physicist in 1920–21. *Ether and Relativity* and *Geometry and Experience*. Elegant ideas in non-mathematical form, accessible to intelligent layman. vi + 56pp. 5⅜ × 8½. 24511-X Pa. $2.95

THE WIT AND HUMOR OF OSCAR WILDE, edited by Alvin Redman. More than 1,000 ripostes, paradoxes, wisecracks: Work is the curse of the drinking classes, I can resist everything except temptation, etc. 258pp. 5⅜ × 8½. 20602-5 Pa. $4.95

ADVENTURES WITH A MICROSCOPE, Richard Headstrom. 59 adventures with clothing fibers, protozoa, ferns and lichens, roots and leaves, much more. 142 illustrations. 232pp. 5⅜ × 8½. 23471-1 Pa. $3.95

PLANTS OF THE BIBLE, Harold N. Moldenke and Alma L. Moldenke. Standard reference to all 230 plants mentioned in Scriptures. Latin name, biblical reference, uses, modern identity, much more. Unsurpassed encyclopedic resource for scholars, botanists, nature lovers, students of Bible. Bibliography. Indexes. 123 black-and-white illustrations. 384pp. 6 × 9. 25069-5 Pa. $8.95

FAMOUS AMERICAN WOMEN: A Biographical Dictionary from Colonial Times to the Present, Robert McHenry, ed. From Pocahontas to Rosa Parks, 1,035 distinguished American women documented in separate biographical entries. Accurate, up-to-date data, numerous categories, spans 400 years. Indices. 493pp. 6½ × 9¼. 24523-3 Pa. $10.95

THE FABULOUS INTERIORS OF THE GREAT OCEAN LINERS IN HISTORIC PHOTOGRAPHS, William H. Miller, Jr. Some 200 superb photographs capture exquisite interiors of world's great "floating palaces"—1890's to 1980's: *Titanic, Ile de France, Queen Elizabeth, United States, Europa,* more. Approx. 200 black-and-white photographs. Captions. Text. Introduction. 160pp. 8⅞ × 11¾. 24756-2 Pa. $9.95

THE GREAT LUXURY LINERS, 1927–1954: A Photographic Record, William H. Miller, Jr. Nostalgic tribute to heyday of ocean liners. 186 photos of Ile de France, Normandie, Leviathan, Queen Elizabeth, United States, many others. Interior and exterior views. Introduction. Captions. 160pp. 9 × 12. 24056-8 Pa. $10.95

A NATURAL HISTORY OF THE DUCKS, John Charles Phillips. Great landmark of ornithology offers complete detailed coverage of nearly 200 species and subspecies of ducks: gadwall, sheldrake, merganser, pintail, many more. 74 full-color plates, 102 black-and-white. Bibliography. Total of 1,920pp. 8⅝ × 11¼. 25141-1, 25142-X Cloth. Two-vol. set $100.00

THE SEAWEED HANDBOOK: An Illustrated Guide to Seaweeds from North Carolina to Canada, Thomas F. Lee. Concise reference covers 78 species. Scientific and common names, habitat, distribution, more. Finding keys for easy identification. 224pp. 5⅜ × 8½. 25215-9 Pa. $6.95

THE TEN BOOKS OF ARCHITECTURE: The 1755 Leoni Edition, Leon Battista Alberti. Rare classic helped introduce the glories of ancient architecture to the Renaissance. 68 black-and-white plates. 336pp. 8⅜ × 11¼. 25239-6 Pa. $14.95

MISS MACKENZIE, Anthony Trollope. Minor masterpieces by Victorian master unmasks many truths about life in 19th-century England. First inexpensive edition in years. 392pp. 5⅜ × 8½. 25201-9 Pa. $8.95

THE RIME OF THE ANCIENT MARINER, Gustave Doré, Samuel Taylor Coleridge. Dramatic engravings considered by many to be his greatest work. The terrifying space of the open sea, the storms and whirlpools of an unknown ocean, the ice of Antarctica, more—all rendered in a powerful, chilling manner. Full text. 38 plates. 77pp. 9¼ × 12. 22305-1 Pa. $4.95

THE EXPEDITIONS OF ZEBULON MONTGOMERY PIKE, Zebulon Montgomery Pike. Fascinating first-hand accounts (1805–6) of exploration of Mississippi River, Indian wars, capture by Spanish dragoons, much more. 1,088pp. 5⅜ × 8½. 25254-X, 25255-8 Pa. Two-vol. set $25.90

A CONCISE HISTORY OF PHOTOGRAPHY: Third Revised Edition, Helmut Gernsheim. Best one-volume history—camera obscura, photochemistry, daguerreotypes, evolution of cameras, film, more. Also artistic aspects—landscape, portraits, fine art, etc. 281 black-and-white photographs. 26 in color. 176pp. 8⅜ × 11¼. 25128-4 Pa. $13.95

THE DORÉ BIBLE ILLUSTRATIONS, Gustave Doré. 241 detailed plates from the Bible: the Creation scenes, Adam and Eve, Flood, Babylon, battle sequences, life of Jesus, etc. Each plate is accompanied by the verses from the King James version of the Bible. 241pp. 9 × 12. 23004-X Pa. $9.95

HUGGER-MUGGER IN THE LOUVRE, Elliot Paul. Second Homer Evans mystery-comedy. Theft at the Louvre involves sleuth in hilarious, madcap caper. "A knockout."—Books. 336pp. 5⅜ × 8½. 25185-3 Pa. $5.95

FLATLAND, E. A. Abbott. Intriguing and enormously popular science-fiction classic explores the complexities of trying to survive as a two-dimensional being in a three-dimensional world. Amusingly illustrated by the author. 16 illustrations. 103pp. 5⅜ × 8½. 20001-9 Pa. $2.50

THE HISTORY OF THE LEWIS AND CLARK EXPEDITION, Meriwether Lewis and William Clark, edited by Elliott Coues. Classic edition of Lewis and Clark's day-by-day journals that later became the basis for U.S. claims to Oregon and the West. Accurate and invaluable geographical, botanical, biological, meteorological and anthropological material. Total of 1,508pp. 5⅜ × 8½.
21268-8, 21269-6, 21270-X Pa. Three-vol. set $26.85

LANGUAGE, TRUTH AND LOGIC, Alfred J. Ayer. Famous, clear introduction to Vienna, Cambridge schools of Logical Positivism. Role of philosophy, elimination of metaphysics, nature of analysis, etc. 160pp. 5⅜ × 8½. (Available in U.S. and Canada only) 20010-8 Pa. $3.95

MATHEMATICS FOR THE NONMATHEMATICIAN, Morris Kline. Detailed, college-level treatment of mathematics in cultural and historical context, with numerous exercises. For liberal arts students. Preface. Recommended Reading Lists. Tables. Index. Numerous black-and-white figures. xvi + 641pp. 5⅜ × 8½.
24823-2 Pa. $11.95

HANDBOOK OF PICTORIAL SYMBOLS, Rudolph Modley. 3,250 signs and symbols, many systems in full; official or heavy commercial use. Arranged by subject. Most in Pictorial Archive series. 143pp. 8⅛ × 11. 23357-X Pa. $6.95

INCIDENTS OF TRAVEL IN YUCATAN, John L. Stephens. Classic (1843) exploration of jungles of Yucatan, looking for evidences of Maya civilization. Travel adventures, Mexican and Indian culture, etc. Total of 669pp. 5⅜ × 8½.
20926-1, 20927-X Pa., Two-vol. set $11.90

DEGAS: An Intimate Portrait, Ambroise Vollard. Charming, anecdotal memoir by famous art dealer of one of the greatest 19th-century French painters. 14 black-and-white illustrations. Introduction by Harold L. Van Doren. 96pp. 5⅜ × 8½.
25131-4 Pa. $4.95

PERSONAL NARRATIVE OF A PILGRIMAGE TO ALMANDINAH AND MECCAH, Richard Burton. Great travel classic by remarkably colorful personality. Burton, disguised as a Moroccan, visited sacred shrines of Islam, narrowly escaping death. 47 illustrations. 959pp. 5⅜ × 8½. 21217-3, 21218-1 Pa., Two-vol. set $19.90

PHRASE AND WORD ORIGINS, A. H. Holt. Entertaining, reliable, modern study of more than 1,200 colorful words, phrases, origins and histories. Much unexpected information. 254pp. 5⅜ × 8½. 20758-7 Pa. $5.95

THE RED THUMB MARK, R. Austin Freeman. In this first Dr. Thorndyke case, the great scientific detective draws fascinating conclusions from the nature of a single fingerprint. Exciting story, authentic science. 320pp. 5⅜ × 8½. (Available in U.S. only) 25210-8 Pa. $6.95

AN EGYPTIAN HIEROGLYPHIC DICTIONARY, E. A. Wallis Budge. Monumental work containing about 25,000 words or terms that occur in texts ranging from 3000 B.C. to 600 A.D. Each entry consists of a transliteration of the word, the word in hieroglyphs, and the meaning in English. 1,314pp. 6⅝ × 10.
23615-3, 23616-1 Pa., Two-vol. set $31.90

THE COMPLEAT STRATEGYST: Being a Primer on the Theory of Games of Strategy, J. D. Williams. Highly entertaining classic describes, with many illustrated examples, how to select best strategies in conflict situations. Prefaces. Appendices. xvi + 268pp. 5⅜ × 8½. 25101-2 Pa. $5.95

THE ROAD TO OZ, L. Frank Baum. Dorothy meets the Shaggy Man, little Button-Bright and the Rainbow's beautiful daughter in this delightful trip to the magical Land of Oz. 272pp. 5⅜ × 8. 25208-6 Pa. $5.95

POINT AND LINE TO PLANE, Wassily Kandinsky. Seminal exposition of role of point, line, other elements in non-objective painting. Essential to understanding 20th-century art. 127 illustrations. 192pp. 6½ × 9¼. 23808-3 Pa. $5.95

LADY ANNA, Anthony Trollope. Moving chronicle of Countess Lovel's bitter struggle to win for herself and daughter Anna their rightful rank and fortune—perhaps at cost of sanity itself. 384pp. 5⅜ × 8½. 24669-8 Pa. $8.95

EGYPTIAN MAGIC, E. A. Wallis Budge. Sums up all that is known about magic in Ancient Egypt: the role of magic in controlling the gods, powerful amulets that warded off evil spirits, scarabs of immortality, use of wax images, formulas and spells, the secret name, much more. 253pp. 5⅜ × 8½. 22681-6 Pa. $4.50

THE DANCE OF SIVA, Ananda Coomaraswamy. Preeminent authority unfolds the vast metaphysic of India: the revelation of her art, conception of the universe, social organization, etc. 27 reproductions of art masterpieces. 192pp. 5⅜ × 8½.
24817-8 Pa. $5.95

CHRISTMAS CUSTOMS AND TRADITIONS, Clement A. Miles. Origin, evolution, significance of religious, secular practices. Caroling, gifts, yule logs, much more. Full, scholarly yet fascinating; non-sectarian. 400pp. 5⅜ × 8½.
23354-5 Pa. $6.95

THE HUMAN FIGURE IN MOTION, Eadweard Muybridge. More than 4,500 stopped-action photos, in action series, showing undraped men, women, children jumping, lying down, throwing, sitting, wrestling, carrying, etc. 390pp. 7⅞ × 10⅝.
20204-6 Cloth. $21.95

THE MAN WHO WAS THURSDAY, Gilbert Keith Chesterton. Witty, fast-paced novel about a club of anarchists in turn-of-the-century London. Brilliant social, religious, philosophical speculations. 128pp. 5⅜ × 8½.
25121-7 Pa. $3.95

A CEZANNE SKETCHBOOK: Figures, Portraits, Landscapes and Still Lifes, Paul Cezanne. Great artist experiments with tonal effects, light, mass, other qualities in over 100 drawings. A revealing view of developing master painter, precursor of Cubism. 102 black-and-white illustrations. 144pp. 8¾ × 6⅝.
24790-2 Pa. $5.95

AN ENCYCLOPEDIA OF BATTLES: Accounts of Over 1,560 Battles from 1479 B.C. to the Present, David Eggenberger. Presents essential details of every major battle in recorded history, from the first battle of Megiddo in 1479 B.C. to Grenada in 1984. List of Battle Maps. New Appendix covering the years 1967–1984. Index. 99 illustrations. 544pp. 6½ × 9¼.
24913-1 Pa. $14.95

AN ETYMOLOGICAL DICTIONARY OF MODERN ENGLISH, Ernest Weekley. Richest, fullest work, by foremost British lexicographer. Detailed word histories. Inexhaustible. Total of 856pp. 6½ × 9¼.
21873-2, 21874-0 Pa., Two-vol. set $17.00

WEBSTER'S AMERICAN MILITARY BIOGRAPHIES, edited by Robert McHenry. Over 1,000 figures who shaped 3 centuries of American military history. Detailed biographies of Nathan Hale, Douglas MacArthur, Mary Hallaren, others. Chronologies of engagements, more. Introduction. Addenda. 1,033 entries in alphabetical order. xi + 548pp. 6½ × 9¼. (Available in U.S. only)
24758-9 Pa. $13.95

LIFE IN ANCIENT EGYPT, Adolf Erman. Detailed older account, with much not in more recent books: domestic life, religion, magic, medicine, commerce, and whatever else needed for complete picture. Many illustrations. 597pp. 5⅜ × 8½.
22632-8 Pa. $8.95

HISTORIC COSTUME IN PICTURES, Braun & Schneider. Over 1,450 costumed figures shown, covering a wide variety of peoples: kings, emperors, nobles, priests, servants, soldiers, scholars, townsfolk, peasants, merchants, courtiers, cavaliers, and more. 256pp. 8⅜ × 11¼.
23150-X Pa. $9.95

THE NOTEBOOKS OF LEONARDO DA VINCI, edited by J. P. Richter. Extracts from manuscripts reveal great genius; on painting, sculpture, anatomy, sciences, geography, etc. Both Italian and English. 186 ms. pages reproduced, plus 500 additional drawings, including studies for *Last Supper, Sforza* monument, etc. 860pp. 7⅞ × 10¾. (Available in U.S. only) 22572-0, 22573-9 Pa., Two-vol. set $31.90

THE ART NOUVEAU STYLE BOOK OF ALPHONSE MUCHA: All 72 Plates from "Documents Decoratifs" in Original Color, Alphonse Mucha. Rare copyright-free design portfolio by high priest of Art Nouveau. Jewelry, wallpaper, stained glass, furniture, figure studies, plant and animal motifs, etc. Only complete one-volume edition. 80pp. 9⅜ × 12¼. 24044-4 Pa. $9.95

ANIMALS: 1,419 COPYRIGHT-FREE ILLUSTRATIONS OF MAMMALS, BIRDS, FISH, INSECTS, ETC., edited by Jim Harter. Clear wood engravings present, in extremely lifelike poses, over 1,000 species of animals. One of the most extensive pictorial sourcebooks of its kind. Captions. Index. 284pp. 9 × 12.
23766-4 Pa. $9.95

OBELISTS FLY HIGH, C. Daly King. Masterpiece of American detective fiction, long out of print, involves murder on a 1935 transcontinental flight—"a very thrilling story"—NY Times. Unabridged and unaltered republication of the edition published by William Collins Sons & Co. Ltd., London, 1935. 288pp. 5⅜ × 8½. (Available in U.S. only) 25036-9 Pa. $5.95

VICTORIAN AND EDWARDIAN FASHION: A Photographic Survey, Alison Gernsheim. First fashion history completely illustrated by contemporary photographs. Full text plus 235 photos, 1840–1914, in which many celebrities appear. 240pp. 6½ × 9¼. 24205-6 Pa. $6.95

THE ART OF THE FRENCH ILLUSTRATED BOOK, 1700–1914, Gordon N. Ray. Over 630 superb book illustrations by Fragonard, Delacroix, Daumier, Doré, Grandville, Manet, Mucha, Steinlen, Toulouse-Lautrec and many others. Preface. Introduction. 633 halftones. Indices of artists, authors & titles, binders and provenances. Appendices. Bibliography. 608pp. 8⅜ × 11¼. 25086-5 Pa. $24.95

THE WONDERFUL WIZARD OF OZ, L. Frank Baum. Facsimile in full color of America's finest children's classic. 143 illustrations by W. W. Denslow. 267pp. 5⅜ × 8½. 20691-2 Pa. $7.95

FRONTIERS OF MODERN PHYSICS: New Perspectives on Cosmology, Relativity, Black Holes and Extraterrestrial Intelligence, Tony Rothman, et al. For the intelligent layman. Subjects include: cosmological models of the universe; black holes; the neutrino; the search for extraterrestrial intelligence. Introduction. 46 black-and-white illustrations. 192pp. 5⅜ × 8½. 24587-X Pa. $7.95

THE FRIENDLY STARS, Martha Evans Martin & Donald Howard Menzel. Classic text marshalls the stars together in an engaging, non-technical survey, presenting them as sources of beauty in night sky. 23 illustrations. Foreword. 2 star charts. Index. 147pp. 5⅜ × 8½. 21099-5 Pa. $3.95

FADS AND FALLACIES IN THE NAME OF SCIENCE, Martin Gardner. Fair, witty appraisal of cranks, quacks, and quackeries of science and pseudoscience: hollow earth, Velikovsky, orgone energy, Dianetics, flying saucers, Bridey Murphy, food and medical fads, etc. Revised, expanded In the Name of Science. "A very able and even-tempered presentation."—The New Yorker. 363pp. 5⅜ × 8.
20394-8 Pa. $6.95

ANCIENT EGYPT: ITS CULTURE AND HISTORY, J. E Manchip White. From pre-dynastics through Ptolemies: society, history, political structure, religion, daily life, literature, cultural heritage. 48 plates. 217pp. 5⅜ × 8½. 22548-8 Pa. $5.95

SIR HARRY HOTSPUR OF HUMBLETHWAITE, Anthony Trollope. Incisive, unconventional psychological study of a conflict between a wealthy baronet, his idealistic daughter, and their scapegrace cousin. The 1870 novel in its first inexpensive edition in years. 250pp. 5⅜ × 8½. 24953-0 Pa. $5.95

LASERS AND HOLOGRAPHY, Winston E. Kock. Sound introduction to burgeoning field, expanded (1981) for second edition. Wave patterns, coherence, lasers, diffraction, zone plates, properties of holograms, recent advances. 84 illustrations. 160pp. 5⅜ × 8¼. (Except in United Kingdom) 24041-X Pa. $3.95

INTRODUCTION TO ARTIFICIAL INTELLIGENCE: SECOND, EN-LARGED EDITION, Philip C. Jackson, Jr. Comprehensive survey of artificial intelligence—the study of how machines (computers) can be made to act intelli-gently. Includes introductory and advanced material. Extensive notes updating the main text. 132 black-and-white illustrations. 512pp. 5⅜ × 8½. 24864-X Pa. $8.95

HISTORY OF INDIAN AND INDONESIAN ART, Ananda K. Coomaraswamy. Over 400 illustrations illuminate classic study of Indian art from earliest Harappa finds to early 20th century. Provides philosophical, religious and social insights. 304pp. 6⅜ × 9⅜. 25005-9 Pa. $9.95

THE GOLEM, Gustav Meyrink. Most famous supernatural novel in modern European literature, set in Ghetto of Old Prague around 1890. Compelling story of mystical experiences, strange transformations, profound terror. 13 black-and-white illustrations. 224pp. 5⅜ × 8½. (Available in U.S. only) 25025-3 Pa. $6.95

PICTORIAL ENCYCLOPEDIA OF HISTORIC ARCHITECTURAL PLANS, DETAILS AND ELEMENTS: With 1,880 Line Drawings of Arches, Domes, Doorways, Facades, Gables, Windows, etc., John Theodore Haneman. Sourcebook of inspiration for architects, designers, others. Bibliography. Captions. 141pp. 9 × 12. 24605-1 Pa. $7.95

BENCHLEY LOST AND FOUND, Robert Benchley. Finest humor from early 30's, about pet peeves, child psychologists, post office and others. Mostly unavailable elsewhere. 73 illustrations by Peter Arno and others. 183pp. 5⅜ × 8½. 22410-4 Pa. $4.95

ERTÉ GRAPHICS, Erté. Collection of striking color graphics: *Seasons, Alphabet, Numerals, Aces* and *Precious Stones.* 50 plates, including 4 on covers. 48pp. 9⅜ × 12¼. 23580-7 Pa. $7.95

THE JOURNAL OF HENRY D. THOREAU, edited by Bradford Torrey, F. H. Allen. Complete reprinting of 14 volumes, 1837–61, over two million words; the sourcebooks for *Walden,* etc. Definitive. All original sketches, plus 75 photographs. 1,804pp. 8½ × 12¼. 20312-3, 20313-1 Cloth., Two-vol. set $120.00

CASTLES: THEIR CONSTRUCTION AND HISTORY, Sidney Toy. Traces castle development from ancient roots. Nearly 200 photographs and drawings illustrate moats, keeps, baileys, many other features. Caernarvon, Dover Castles, Hadrian's Wall, Tower of London, dozens more. 256pp. 5⅜ × 8¼. 24898-4 Pa. $6.95

AMERICAN CLIPPER SHIPS: 1833–1858, Octavius T. Howe & Frederick C. Matthews. Fully-illustrated, encyclopedic review of 352 clipper ships from the period of America's greatest maritime supremacy. Introduction. 109 halftones. 5 black-and-white line illustrations. Index. Total of 928pp. 5⅜ × 8½.
25115-2, 25116-0 Pa., Two-vol. set $17.90

TOWARDS A NEW ARCHITECTURE, Le Corbusier. Pioneering manifesto by great architect, near legendary founder of "International School." Technical and aesthetic theories, views on industry, economics, relation of form to function, "mass-production spirit," much more. Profusely illustrated. Unabridged translation of 13th French edition. Introduction by Frederick Etchells. 320pp. 6⅛ × 9¼. (Available in U.S. only)
25023-7 Pa. $8.95

THE BOOK OF KELLS, edited by Blanche Cirker. Inexpensive collection of 32 full-color, full-page plates from the greatest illuminated manuscript of the Middle Ages, painstakingly reproduced from rare facsimile edition. Publisher's Note. Captions. 32pp. 9⅜ × 12¼.
24345-1 Pa. $4.95

BEST SCIENCE FICTION STORIES OF H. G. WELLS, H. G. Wells. Full novel *The Invisible Man*, plus 17 short stories: "The Crystal Egg," "Aepyornis Island," "The Strange Orchid," etc. 303pp. 5⅜ × 8½. (Available in U.S. only)
21531-8 Pa. $6.95

AMERICAN SAILING SHIPS: Their Plans and History, Charles G. Davis. Photos, construction details of schooners, frigates, clippers, other sailcraft of 18th to early 20th centuries—plus entertaining discourse on design, rigging, nautical lore, much more. 137 black-and-white illustrations. 240pp. 6⅛ × 9¼.
24658-2 Pa. $6.95

ENTERTAINING MATHEMATICAL PUZZLES, Martin Gardner. Selection of author's favorite conundrums involving arithmetic, money, speed, etc., with lively commentary. Complete solutions. 112pp. 5⅜ × 8½.
25211-6 Pa. $2.95

THE WILL TO BELIEVE, HUMAN IMMORTALITY, William James. Two books bound together. Effect of irrational on logical, and arguments for human immortality. 402pp. 5⅜ × 8½.
20291-7 Pa. $7.95

THE HAUNTED MONASTERY and THE CHINESE MAZE MURDERS, Robert Van Gulik. 2 full novels by Van Gulik continue adventures of Judge Dee and his companions. An evil Taoist monastery, seemingly supernatural events; overgrown topiary maze that hides strange crimes. Set in 7th-century China. 27 illustrations. 328pp. 5⅜ × 8½.
23502-5 Pa. $6.95

CELEBRATED CASES OF JUDGE DEE (DEE GOONG AN), translated by Robert Van Gulik. Authentic 18th-century Chinese detective novel; Dee and associates solve three interlocked cases. Led to Van Gulik's own stories with same characters. Extensive introduction. 9 illustrations. 237pp. 5⅜ × 8½.
23337-5 Pa. $4.95

Prices subject to change without notice.
Available at your book dealer or write for free catalog to Dept. GI, Dover Publications, Inc., 31 East 2nd St., Mineola, N.Y. 11501. Dover publishes more than 175 books each year on science, elementary and advanced mathematics, biology, music, art, literary history, social sciences and other areas.